INDUSTRIAL PHARMACY I

DR. SHIKHA BAGHEL CHAUHAN & DR. INDU SINGH

Contents

Preface

This textbook of Industrial Pharmacy I (B. Pharm V Semester) enables the student to understand and appreciate the influence of pharmaceutical additives and various pharmaceutical dosage forms on the performance of the drug product. The book provides detailed insight into the various pharmaceutical dosage forms and their manufacturing techniques. It also helps in understanding the various considerations in development of pharmaceutical dosage forms. The book provides various techniques of formulation solid, liquid and semisolid dosage forms and their evaluation, methods for assessment of their quality. It covers all the topics as prescribed in the latest syllabus prescribed by PCI including Preformulation Studies, Tablets, Liquid orals, Hard gelatin capsules, soft gelatin capsules, Pellets, Parenteral Products, Ophthalmic Preparations, Cosmetics, Pharmaceutical Aerosols and Packaging Materials Sciences.

Acknowledgements

It is our immense pleasure to publish and present this book of Industrial Pharmacy I (B.Pharm V Semester) to the pharmaceutical sciences students, teachers, and research scholars.

Any successful outcome is not an individual effort, but it is a joint venture of many people who put in their mind and soul for the completion of the work. We would like to acknowledge the extraordinary debt we owe to our dear students **Amisha Chauhan, Sakshi Nainwani, Muskan Sethi, Umang Parashar, Astha Singh, Akshat Mahajan, Sanskriti Gupta, Bhavika Puri and Stuti Singh.** We would never have been able, to complete this book without their support and motivation.

We are highly thankful to our Director (Amity Institute of Pharmacy, Amity University, Noida), **Dr. Sandeep Arorasir**, for his support, motivation, and constant encouragement. We hope this book will help the students in understanding the core concepts of subject and develop deep understanding of subject.

The readers of this book are requested to present their reviews and suggestions which will be highly appreciated and accepted by the authors. Constructive suggestions, comments and criticism on the subject matter of the book will be gratefully acknowledged, as they will certainly help to improve future editions of the book.

CHAPTER I

PREFORMULATION STUDIES

INTRODUCTION

We must first understand the drug's properties and potency in comparison to competing products, as well as conduct a literature search for stability and decay data, the proposed route of drug administration, and a literature survey for formulation approaches, bioavailability, and pharmacokinetics of chemically related drugs, before beginning preformulation studies. Once a pharmacologically active molecule has been identified, it is the responsibility of a multidisciplinary project team to ensure that molecule enters the development process in the best possible molecular form. Probing experiments should be conducted out after the first good sample of a new medication is obtained to determine the size of each identified issue region. If a flaw is found, the project team should figure out which chemical alterations are most likely to improve the drug's qualities[1]. Salts, prodrugs, solvates, polymorphs, and even novel analogues could result from these alterations.

Preformulation is the process of a novel drug entity interfering with formulation development. Preformulation is the process of developing an effective drug delivery system based on the physicochemical features of a treatment using biopharmaceutical concepts. Preformulation studies are an important technique in the early phases of API and medicinal product development. The interaction of the drug component and excipients is investigated in the preformulation study. The ICH, including the US FDA's IND, NDA, and ANDA guidelines, encouraged preformulation studies. Preformulation studies were designed to provide all necessary data (especially physicochemical, physicomechanical, and biopharmaceutical properties of drug substances, excipients, and packaging materials) that influenced formulation design, manufacturing method, and final product pharmacokinetic/ biopharmaceutical properties[3]. Drugs that are designed to achieve a prolonged therapeutic effect by continuously releasing medication over an extended period of time after a single dose have been administered are referred to as sustained release, sustained action, controlled release, extended action, timed release, depot, and repository dosage forms. The term "sustained release" has long been used to refer to a pharmacological dose form that slows the release of a medicament[4].

Differential Scanning Preformulation experiments on zidovudine derivatives were conducted using calorimetry, thermography, X-Ray Powder Diffractometry, and aqueous stability tests..

It's defined as a study of a pharmaceutical ingredient's physical and chemical qualities on its own and in conjunction with excipients. **The overall purpose of preformulation testing is to offer information that will help the formulator create stable and bioavailable dosage forms that can be mass produced.** Preformulation studies should include physicochemical, physico-mechanical, and biological properties of medicinal components, excipients, and packaging materials. During the early synthesis of a new pharmaceutical molecule, the synthetic chemist may record some data that can be considered preformulation data, either alone or in collaboration with professionals in other domains, including preformulation. The earliest stage of learning is referred to as pre- formulation. Pre-formulation is the process of applying biopharmaceutical principles to a pharmacological substance's physicochemical qualities in order to create the best potential drug delivery system[5].

Preformulation during Drug Discovery

Preformulation studies aid in the identification of leads during the drug discovery phase, in addition to assisting with formulation development. To become a medicine molecule, a novel chemical entity must have ideal biopharmaceutical qualities[6]. Possessing potency and selectivity alone does not imply 'drug ability.' Preformulation studies aid in determining a molecule's 'drug ability.' As a result, preformulation can be viewed as a crucial decision-making tool during both the drug research and development phases. A deep understanding of physicochemical features and their impact on biological performance allows for the identification of possible lead compounds as well as drug delivery difficulties[7].

Scientists can use preformulation to screen lead candidates based on their physicochemical and biological qualities. This data or collected source can help with the identification of new chemical entities (NCEs) for preclinical efficacy/toxicity investigations, which is an important part of the investigational new drug application process. In order to lower attrition rate in late stage development, a strong collaboration between the discovery and formulation groups is required for identifying the proper NCEs[6].

The nature and substance of the formulations will vary depending on the stage of development, but the formulation chosen for full-scale clinical trials should be as close to the final product as possible. Otherwise, comprehensive clinical comparison trials may be required to show that the formulation utilized in the clinical trials and the formulation proposed for subsequent marketing are identical[8]. Pre-formulation studies should be conducted not only to evaluate the characteristics of candidate drugs but also potential formulation excipients and their interactions with drug substances, in order to select appropriate formulation ingredients, to ensure that the various formulations are optimized for their intended use. Furthermore, preformulation studies should analyze the effect of different preparation, manufacturing, and storage circumstances on stability, in order to provide assurance that a reliable assessment of the candidate medicine was undertaken during development and in routine, post-marketing use[9].

OBJECTIVE OF PREFORMULATION[11]

- Before developing elegant dosage forms (that are stable, effective, and safe).
- It is necessary to have a thorough understanding of the physical description of the pharmacological substance.
- It is the first phase in the logical creation of a drug substance's dosage form prior to dosage form development.
- It provides knowledgeable information for the formulator to construct an optimal drug delivery system.
- It is used to formulate or develop elegant dosage forms.
- Physico-chemical properties of a new drug entity must be established.
- Its kinetics and stability must be determined.
- To see whether it's compatible with commonly used excipients
- It explains how drug items should be prepared and stored in order to maintain their quality.
- The preformulation studies show that there are no significant obstacles to the chemical becoming a commercial medication. These details are used by the formulation scientist to create dosage forms.
- A drug candidate's preformulation is a multidisciplinary development process.
- To provide useful information to the formulator; to improve drug stability; to eliminate excipient incompatibility; and to boost drug bioavailability.

GOAL OF PREFORMULATION

- Physico-chemical parameters of a new medicinal compound must be established
- To determine the physical traits of a person
- The goal is to create a kinetic rate profile
- To determine whether or not the common excipient is compatible
- To select the proper dosage form of a pharmacological compound

IMPORTANCE OF PREFORMULATION[12]

- To supply accurate drugs in a safe, effective, and convenient manner
- To guard against harmful environmental factors such as oxygen and humidity
- To protect against gastric acid and to have an impact following oral intake. Take, for example, an enteric-coated tablet
- To mask the odour and flavor of the medicine
- To provide a liquid preparation that is unstable or insoluble solubility and stability. Suspension is an example

- To give controlled pharmacological action at a rate. Aspirin, for example, is a sustained release and controlled release tablet.
- It refers to the process of improving medication delivery by determining the physical and chemical features of new drug molecules that influence therapeutic performance and developing an effective, stable, and safe dosage form.
- Preformulation research on a new therapeutic molecule can help with the formulation of a physicochemically stable and biopharmaceutically appropriate dose form later on.

MAJOR AREAS OF PREFORMULATION STUDIES

Some of the major preformulation studies are as follow in figure:1

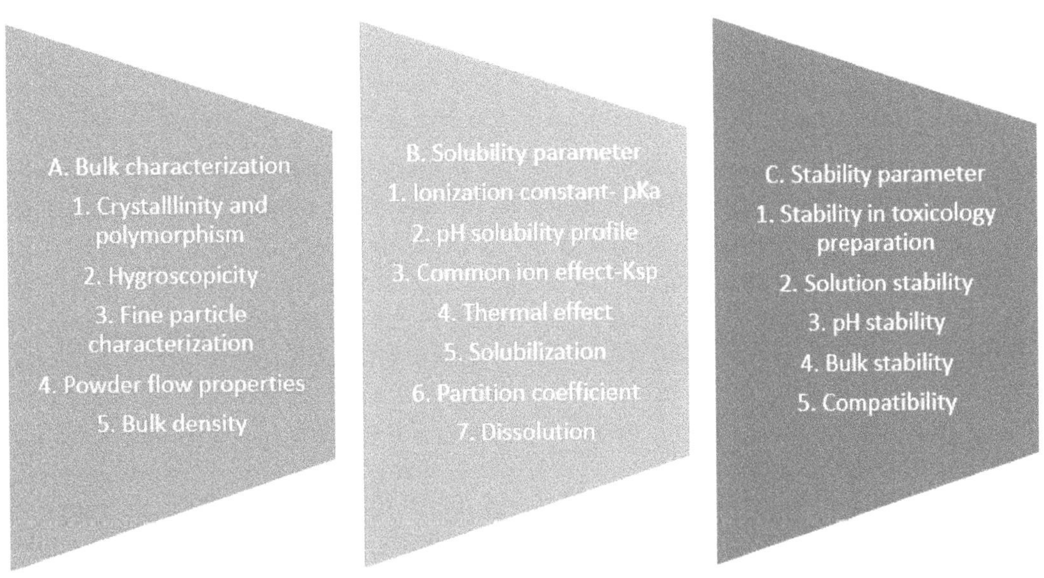

Figure 1 Preformulation Studies

A. BULK CHARACTERIZATION

Almost every solid form of a drug is subject to bulk characterization. The downstream formulation process is influenced by particle size, bulk density, and surface shape, as well as flow ability, strength, and agglomeration strength. To avoid making inaccurate assumptions about stability or solubility, every preformulation bulk lots must be thoroughly characterized. It is necessary to identify all solid forms that may exist as a result of the synthesis stage, such as the presence of polymorphs. To avoid misleading predictions of solubility and stability that are based on a specific crystalline form, bulk characteristics such as particle size, bulk density, and surface morphology may be changed throughout the development phase. During evolution of a process, bulk parameters for solid forms such as particle size, bulk density, and surface morphology are likely to change[13].

Crystallinity refers to the degree of structural organization in a solid. Internal structure and crystal habit of the medication can affect bulk and physicochemical properties. The molecular arrangement within the solid is described by the internal structure, and changes in the internal structure usually occur after the crystalline habit has been established. The majority of pharmaceuticals are found in a solid state. Few are liquids, such as valproic acid, and even fewer are gases, such as some general anaesthetics. In a crystal, a crystal structure is a unique arrangement of atoms. Physical qualities influenced by solid-state features can influence both the delivery system chosen and the drug's activity, as defined by the rate of delivery. Chemical stability can be influenced significantly by physical attributes the exterior and internal structures of a crystalline particle are distinct. The outward shape of a crystal is described by crystal habit, whereas the polymorphic state refers to the definite arrangement of molecules within the crystal lattice. The final step in the purification of a solid is almost always crystallization. Different solvents and processing conditions can change the behavior of recrystallized particles as well as the solid's polymorphic state[14]. The structure of a solid compound is referred to as crystallinity, and these structures vanish in the liquid and vapour stages. Internal structures can be classed as cubic, tetragonal, hexagonal, rhombic, and so on. Unbreakable habits (platy, needle, tabular, prismatic, bladed, and so on), Changing the interior structure has an impact on crystal habits, while changing the chemical form (such as salt formation) has an impact on both the internal structure and crystal habit. Polymorphs are formed through crystallisation from various solvents and solidification after melting. When the integrated solvent is water, it's called "hydrates." The term "anhydrous" refers to a chemical that does not contain any water in its crystal structure[15].

.

1. **Polymorphismand crystallization**

It refers to a compound's ability to crystallize as multiple separate crystalline species, each with its own internal Latin. Many physiochemical properties of solids, such as melting point, density, hardness, crystal form, optical property, and solubility, are affected by their internal structure. Many drugs can exist in several crystalline forms, each with a different space lattice configuration. Polymorphism is the term for this characteristic. Polymorphs refer to the various crystal formations. When polymorphism occurs, the molecules in the crystal organize themselves in two or more different ways; they may be packed differently in the crystal lattice or the orientation or conformation of the molecules at the lattice sites may differ. In three dimensions, atoms in crystalline materials are arranged in regular and recurring patterns. In amorphous substances, for example, atoms or molecules are randomly distributed without a regular atomic order. Polymorphism refers to a compound's ability to crystallize as multiple unique crystalline species, each having a different internal lattice and different crystal shapes (at different free energy states). Melting point, density, vapor pressure X-ray, color, crystal structure, hardness, solubility, dissolution rate, and bioavailability are all diverse physicochemical qualities[17]. Poor free energy, low solubility, and a high melting point characterize stable polymorphs[18].

With higher solubility and bioavailability and a lower melting point, the metastable polymorph is less stable. Microscopy, thermal analysis, and the X-ray diffraction method are used to analyze crystals and polymorphs. Solubility and stability can have an impact on the significance of crystal shape and internal structure identification.. Powder flow characteristics are influenced by density and crystal structure. The compression properties and grinding operations of tablets are influenced by their hardness[19].

Polymorphism types[20]

Enantiotropic polymorphisms can be turned back into one another by changing temperature and pressure. Sulfur, carbon, nitrogen, and oxygen, for example.

Monotropic Polymorphism that is unstable at all temperatures and pressures. Glyceryl stearate, for example.

PSUEDO POLYMORPHISM- The word "pseudo" literally means "false." Solvates are phenomena in which solvent molecules are integrated into the crystal lattice of a solid. Pseudopolymorphism is phenomena in which solvates exist in multiple crystal forms called pseudopolymorphs. When water is the solvent, it is also known as hydrates. Four distinct crystalline solvates are generated when the powerful synthetic oestrogen 'ethynyle- stradiol' is crystallized from the solvents acetonitrile, methanol, chloroform, and saturated with water. By employing hot stage microscopy to observe melting behavior in silicon oil, pseudo-polymorphs can be distinguished from actual polymorphs. Pseudo polymorphs emit gas (steam or solvent vapors) in this process, causing the oil to bubble. True polymorphs, on the other hand, simply melt and generate a second globular phase[21,22]

METHOD USED FOR IDENTIFYING POLYMORPHISM

i. Microscopy

Microscopy is a branch of science that involves using microscopes to examine items and parts of objects that are not visible to the human eye [1] Optical, electron, and scanning probe microscopy are the three most well-known branches of microscopy, with X-ray microscopy being a newer branch. When examined under a microscope with crossed polarizing filters, almost all transparent substances are either isotropic or anisotropic. Isotropic materials have a single refractive index, such as amorphous solids and non-crystalline solid organic molecules. When a plain polarized filter passes through these isotropic substances, they do not transmit light and appear black[23].

Anisotropic materials have many refractive indices and glow on a dark polarized background. The thickness of the crystals and their refractive indices determine color interference. Anisotropy can be uniaxial or biaxial. To construct or characterize the complete crystal shape, a crystallographic axe is necessary. Polymorphism, melting points, transition temperatures, and transition rates can all be studied at a controlled rate using a polarizing microscope with a heated stage[24,25].

v. TEM:

A TEM is a technique for photographing the precise structure of a drug molecule. It is possible to attain a total magnification of roughly 20 million times and view things as small as 2nm. The TEM penetrates the drug's surface and reveals the drug's internal structure[26].

v. Fusion method

When the carrier is heated just above its melting point in this fusion process, the drug is integrated into a matrix. After that, the mixture is refrigerated and regularly mixed. Cool the dispersion to room temperature gradually or fast in an ice bath. The fusion approach is also known as the hot-melt method. This term can only be used when the starting material is crystalline. After the dispersion has cooled, the finished product is crushed and sieved. When the components are blended using an extrusion process, the method is known as the hot melt extrusion method[27]

v. DSC (Differential Scanning Calorimetry)

Throughout the experiment, the sample and reference are kept at nearly the same temperature. The temperature programme for a DSC study is usually set up so that the sample holder temperature rises linearly as time passes. Over the temperature range to be scanned, the reference sample should have a well-defined heat capacity. It involves certain adjustments to the thermocouple sensor's location as well as maintaining a consistent heat lux to the sample. DSC can also be used to describe a sample's physical and chemical properties. Heat flux and power compensated are two types of DSC[28].

v. IR (Infrared spectroscopy)

Infrared spectroscopy (IR spectroscopy) is a type of spectroscopy that studies light in the infrared spectrum, which has a longer wavelength and lower frequency than visible light. It includes a variety of approaches, the majority of which are based on absorption spectroscopy. It may be used to identify and analyze compounds, just like any other spectroscopic approach. It works on the basis of absorption spectroscopy. Infrared spectroscopy is a process or technique that produces an infrared spectrum using an instrument called an infrared spectrometer[29].

v. X-Ray Powder Diffraction (XRPD):

X-ray powder diffraction (XRD) is a quick analytical technique that can offer information on unit cell dimensions and is mostly used for phase identification of crystalline materials. The studied material is finely powdered and homogenized, and the bulk composition is calculated on an average basis[30].

v. **SEM**

A scanning electron microscope (SEM) is a type of electron microscope that uses a concentrated beam of electrons to scan the surface of a sample to obtain images. When electrons contact with atoms in a sample, they produce a variety of signals that provide information about the sample's surface topography and composition. SEM is a technique for examining the surface of a pharmacological molecule. An electron beam is blasted from an electron gun and rapidly sweeps across the specimen's surface, scanning the drug's surface in this type of microscopy. SEM is used to examine the drug molecule's surface. In this microscopy, the electron beam is conveyed from an electron cannon that rapidly passes over the specimen's surface. This causes a secondary electron shower to be emitted, as well as other forms of changes, allowing the drug's surface to be examined[31].

v. **Thermo-gravimetric Analysis:**

Thermo-gravimetric analysis, often known as thermal gravimetric analysis (TGA), is a type of thermal analysis that measures changes in a material's physical and chemical properties. As a function of temperature or physical processes such as second order phase transitions such as vaporization, sublimation, absorption, and adsorption and desorption. Thermogravimetric analysis (TGA) is an analytical technique that monitors the weight change that occurs as a sample is heated at a constant pace to assess a material's thermal stability and fraction of volatile components[32].

2. **HYGROSCOPICITY**

Hygroscopic refers to a substance that collects enough moisture from the air. Many pharmacological compounds, particularly water-soluble salt versions, have a proclivity for absorbing moisture from the environment. According to Van Campen, air humidity, temperature, surface area, exposure, and the method of moisture uptake can all affect adsorption and equilibrium moisture content. Some compounds, such as sodium chloride, absorb enough water to dissolve fully in a humid climate. Because of hydrate production, other hygroscopic compounds adsorb water. Bulk medication samples are placed in open containers with a thin powder layer to ensure maximal ambient exposure for testing for hygroscopicity. After that, the samples are exposed to a variety of regulated relative humidity settings made from saturated aqueous salt solution. The sample's moisture uptake can be measured at various stages of handle (0 to 24 hours) and storing of sample (0 to 12 weeks). Gravimetric analysis, thermo gravimetric analysis, Karl Fischer titration, and gas chromatography are all analytical procedures for detecting moisture levels.

Moisture is another component that can have an impact on the stability of candidate medications and their formulations. Hydrolysis is frequently induced by the sorption of water molecules onto a potential medication (or excipient).

DIFFERENT CLASSES OF HYGROSCOPIC SUBSTANCES

CLASS 1- NON-HYGOSCOPIC- At relative humidity below 90%, there are almost no moisture increases.

CLASS 2- SLIGHTLY HYGROSCOPIC- At relative humidity levels below 80%, almost no moisture is present.

CLASS 3- MODERATELY HYGROSCOPIC- After a week of storage at a relative humidity of less than 60%, the moisture content does not increase by more than 5%.

CLASS 4- VERY HYGROSCOPIC- At relative humidity levels as low as 40 to 50 percent, moisture content can rise.

To determine hygroscopicity, bulk medication samples are placed in open containers with a thin powder layer to ensure maximal exposure to the atmosphere. After that, the samples are placed in a controlled relative humidity environment made up of saturated aqueous salt solutions. Moisture uptake should be measured at various handling intervals (0 to 24 hours) and storage times (0 to 12 weeks). The precision sought and the amount of moisture adsorbed on the drug sample determine the analytical methods for measuring the moisture level (i.e. gravimetery, TGA, or gas chromatography)[34].

3. FINE PARTICLE CHARACTERIZATION

Size has a direct impact on bulk flow, formulation uniformity, and surface area controlled processes including dissolution and chemical reactivity. The drug particle's shape and surface morphology. Each novel medicine should be tested prior to preformulation. The lowest particle size possible was used in the tests make it easier to prepare homogeneous samples and maximize the surface area of the medication for interactions. A light microscope with a calibrated grid is typically sufficient for determining the form and size of drug particles. To get typical dispersion, careful sampling and preparation of microscope slides is required[36].

Photomicrographs and a hemacytometer slide, as well as other size techniques, could make this work a little easier. Coulter counter analysis samples are made by scattering the material in a conducting medium, such as isotonic saline, with the help of ultrasound and a few drops of surfactant. The volume of the suspension is determined, and then voltage is applied across this region by drowning it in a tube through a tiny hole. Counted the number of passes through the hole depending on the size acc. because each particle is unique. To the resistance created by moving the conducting media volume of that particle. Big samples of fairly large particles (100 microns or greater) are often sampled using sieves[35].

Drugs have certain physical and chemical features. The particle size has an impact on chemicals distribution, including the rate of drug dissolution, bioavailability, consistency of content, taste, and texture, color, and consistency Furthermore, features such as among other things, flow characteristics and sedimentation rates Others are also crucial particle-related factors. size. Methods of particle size and dispersion evaluation features a light microscope with a grid that can be calibrated, Stream scanning, sedimentation approaches Surface area measurement with a Coulter counter. The BET nitrogen adsorption method is a method for adsorbing nitrogen[37,38].

Brunauer, Emmett, and Teller (BET) nitrogen adsorption, in which a coating of nitrogen molecules is adsorbed to the sample surface at -1960C, provides a more precise measurement of surface area. The sample is heated to room temperature, the nitrogen gas is desorbed, and its volume is determined and translated to the number of adsorbed molecules using the ideal gas law[39]. Scanning electron microscopy (SEM) can be used to examine surface morphology, which helps to corroborate qualitatively a physical observation about surface area. Bulk amounts of medication recovered using various crystallization procedures in an attempt to boost yield, for example, may have surface morphologies that provide more surface area for surface interactions such as degradation, dissolution, or hygroscopicity[40].

4. POWDER FLOW CHARACTERISTICS

To ensure efficient mixing and acceptable weight homogeneity for the compressed tablets, a good flow of the powder or granulation to be compressed is required. If a medicine is found to be "poorly flowable" during the preformulation stage, the problem can be remedied by using the right excipients. To improve flow characteristics, medication powders may need to be pre-compressed or granulated in some circumstances. Angle of repose, flow through an orifice, compressibility index, shear cell, and other methods are among them. Particle size and shape changes are usually obvious; a larger crystal size or a more uniform shape will result in a narrower angle of repose and a lower Carr's index. Pharmaceutical powders can be categorized as either free-flowing or cohesive (non-free flowing). Changes in particle size, density, shape, electrostatic charge, and adsorbed moisture that occur during processing or formulation have a substantial impact on most flow properties[41].

In a variety of sectors of research, angle of repose has been utilized to characterize the flow properties of solids. Angle of repose is used to assess inter particulate friction, or the resistance to movement between particles. As the cone is formed, material segregation and consolidation or aeration of the powder cause experimental issues. Table 1 consist of range of angle of repose with respect to flow property[42].

Formula used for angle of repose: tanØ= height/base

FLOW PROPERTY	ANGLE OF REPOSE	COMPRESSIBILITY INDEX (5%)	HAUSNER's RATIO
Excellent	25-30	≤10	1.00-1.11
Good	31-35	11-15	1.12-1.18
Fair-aid not needed	36-40	16-20	1.19-1.25
Passable-may hang up	41-45	21-25	1.26-1.34
Poor-must agitate, vibrate	46-55	26-31	1.35-1.45
Very poor	56-65	32-37	1.46-1.59
Very, very poor	>66	>38	>1.60

Table 1: Angle of Repose

Compressibility index and Hausner's ratio: The compressibility index, as well as the closely related Hausner's ratio, have become prominent tools for forecasting powder flow characteristics in recent years. Both the bulk volume and the tapped volume of powder are measured to obtain the compressibility index and the Hausner's ratio[43].

Using measured values for bulk density and tapped density, the compressibility index and Hausner's ratio can be calculated as follows:

Compressibility Index =Tapped density- bulk density/tapped density*100

Hausner's ratio=tapped density/bulk density

5. **BULK DENSITY**

Soil compaction is measured by bulk density. It's computed by dividing the dry weight of the soil by its volume. The volume of soil particles as well as the volume of pores between soil particles are included in this volume. The density of bulk material is usually measured in grams per cubic meters. The mass to volume ratio of an untouched powder sample determines the bulk density of the powder. It is taken into account the contribution of the inter particle void volume. As a result, powder particle bulk density and spatial organization in the powder bed are critical. Bulk density is measurement in graduated cylinder, volumeter, vessles[44].

B. **<u>SOLUBILITY PARAMETER</u>**

Preformulation solubility studies concentrate on the drug solvent system that may arise during the delivery candidate, such as a medicine for oral administration. Solubility in isotonic media was investigated with concentration of chloride ions and acidic pH of 26. Typically, preformulation solubility investigations involve pH, temperature dependency, pka determination solubility profile, solubilization of solubility products, Analytical technique for processes and rate of dissolution they are particularly functional for determining solubility HPLC,

UV, Spectroscopy, and Fluorescence, Gas chromatography and spectroscopy. For the majority of drugs, reverse phase HPLC is a cost-effective and precise method of separation a method of gathering data on solubility. Solubility and dissolution factors should be defined by pH, temperature, ionic strength, and buffer concentration. Solubility, particularly water solubility, is an important physical-chemical property of a medicinal substance[45].

For therapeutic efficacy in the physiological pH range of 1 to 8, a medication must have some water solubility. A drug must first be in solution form before it may enter systemic circulation and exhibit therapeutic effect. If the solubility of a drug material is less than optimum, it should be considered increasing its solubility. There may be incomplete or unpredictable absorption over pH ranges 1-7 at 37°C due to poor solubility (10mg/ml).One of the main goals of the preformulation effort is to develop a method for producing medication solutions. For therapeutic efficacy, a medication must have some aqueous solubility. A drug must first be in solution before it may penetrate the systemic circulation and exhibit a therapeutic effect. Incomplete absorption is common with somewhat insoluble substances. When a solute dissolve, the intermolecular forces of attraction of the material must be overcome by forces of attraction between the solute and solvent molecules[46]. The solute solute forces and the solvent-solvent forces must be broken to achieve the solute solvent attraction. It focuses on drug-solvent interactions that may occur during the distribution of drug candidates. Drugs that are taken orally should be evaluated for solubility in a simulated stomach medium. The solubility analysis of a novel medicine is essential to lay the groundwork for subsequent formulation work and can have an impact on the drug's performance. Bioabsorption will be problematic for drugs with an aqueous solubility of less than 1% (10 mg/ml). Temperature, chemical and physical properties of both the solute and the solvent, pressure, solution acidity or basicity, state of subdivision of the solute and solvent, physical agitation imparted to the solution during the dissolving process, and other factors all play a role in the dissolving process[47]. Solubility as per USP are given in Table 2.

TABLE 2: SOLUBIILITY AS PER USP[48]

DESCRIPTION	PART OF SOLVENT REQUIRED FOR 1 PART OF SOLUTE
Very soluble	Less than 1
Freely soluble	From 1 to 10
Soluble	From 1 to 30
Sparingly soluble	From 30 to 100
Slightly soluble	From 100 to 1,000
Very slightly soluble	From 1,000 to 10,000
Practically insoluble	10,000 and above

TABLE 2: SOLUBIILITY AS PER USP

1. **Constant (PKa Determination) Ionization**

The dissociation constant for a medication capable of ionization within a pH range of 1 to 10 must be determined. Because solubility and, as a result, absorption can vary by orders of magnitude when pH changes. The Henderson-Hasselbalch equation calculates the ionized and un-ionized drug concentrations at a given pH.

FOR ACIDIC COMPOUND= pH= pKa + log ionized drug/ unionized drug

FOR BASIC COMPOUND= pH= pKa + log unionized drug/ionized drug

The un-ionized form of a weekly acidic drug with a pKa value > 3 is present in the acidic content of the stomach, but the ionized form is predominately in the neutral media of the intestine. For basic drugs such as erythromycin and papaverine (pKa 8 to 9), the ionized form is predominant in both the stomach and intestine. A variety of analytical procedures can be used to determine pKa values. The pKa value is affected by buffer, temperature, ionic strength, and co-solvent. Method for determination of PKA are Potentiometric Titration, Spectrophotometric Determination, Dissolution rate method, Liquid-Liquid Partition method[49].

Significance

1.The solubility at any pH can be predicted if the inherent solubility and pKa are known.

2.Henderson equations can help you choose the right salt-forming chemicals and anticipate their solubility.

3.The ratio of an ionized to a unionized form of a medicinal molecule is calculated. This can be used to forecast which form will dominate at certain physiologic pH levels. The unionized form of the medication is most commonly absorbed. As a result, acidic medications will be absorbed in the stomach's acidic medium, and vice versa[50].

Method of determination of dissociation constant

HPLC: HPLC (high-performance liquid chromatography), formerly known as high-pressure liquid chromatography, is an analytical chemistry technique for separating, identifying, and quantifying each component in a mixture. Pumps are used to move a pressured liquid solvent containing the sample combination through a solid adsorbent material-filled column. Each component in the sample interacts with the adsorbent material in a slightly different way, resulting in varying flow rates and separation of the components as they flow out of the column[51].

Hyper Rayleigh scattering

Hyper–Rayleigh scattering is a type of scattering that occurs when a particle Optical Activity (/reli/ RAY-lee) is a nonlinear optical physical effect in which chiral scatterers (such as nanoparticles or molecules) convert light (or other electromagnetic radiation) to higher frequencies via harmonic generation processes, with the intensity of generated light being dependent on the chirality of the scatterers. The nonlinear optical analogue of Rayleigh scattering is "hyper–Rayleigh scattering." Any variations in light attributes (such as intensity or polarization) caused by chirality are referred to as "optical activity."[52]

Calorimetery

Calorimetry methods all operate on the same principle: a physical or chemical reaction occurs in a sample, and the amount of heat released is measured. In isothermal titration Calorimetry (ITC), a typical acid-base titration is carried out inside the calorimeter while the energy necessary to maintain a constant temperature is determined[53].

UV Visible spectroscopy

It is the study of absorption and reflectance spectroscopy in the ultraviolet and nearby visible parts of the electromagnetic spectrum. This means it makes use of visible and neighbouring light. The color of the substances involved is directly affected by their absorption or reflectance in the visual spectrum. Atoms and molecules undergo electronic transitions in this region of the spectrum. Absorption spectroscopy is similar to fluorescence spectroscopy in that it measures transitions from the ground state to the excited state, whereas fluorescence measures transitions from the excited state to the ground state[54].

Density Functional Theory (Dfi) Method

The computational method is density functional theory. DFI is now one of the most widely used methods for determining pKa values. Science to study the electronic structure (or nuclear structure) of many-body systems, particularly atoms, molecules, and condensed phases (principally the ground state). The features of a many-electron system can be determined using functionals, or functions of other functions, according to this theory. These are the functionals of the spatially dependent electron density in DFT. In condensed-matter physics, computational physics, and computational chemistry, DFT is one of the most common and adaptable approaches[55].

Isohydric Solution Principle

This approach is extremely sensitive, making it ideal for weak acids with low pKa values. The isohydric principle describes phenomena in which several acid/base pairs in solution are in equilibrium with one another due to a common reagent: the hydrogen ion, which determines the pH of the solution. When many buffers are combined in a solution, they are all exposed to the same hydrogen ion activity. As a result, according to the Henderson-Hasselbalch equation, the pK of each buffer determines the ratio of the concentrations of its base and weak acid forms at a particular pH[56]. The equation used for determining pKa is-

C = C+ C2. 10PK1T

Solvation method

Ions are surrounded by a concentric shell of solvent during the solvation process. The process of rearranging solvent and solute molecules into solvation complexes is known as solvation. Bond formation, hydrogen bonding, and van der Waals forces are all involved in solvation. Hydration is the process of a solute being dissolved in water[57].

Thermal Lensing Spectroscopy

Thermal Lens Spectroscopy (TLS) is a type of fluorimetry that measures the effects of molecules relaxing in their excited states. Fluorimetry is a highly sensitive analytical technique. a portable Diode-laser/fiber-optic thermal lense spectroscopy consisting of a visible diode laser, a photodiode, and an optical fibre was used to detect the dissociation constant of thymol blue[58].

Flourimetric Method

Flourimetry is a quick and accurate method for evaluating the dissociation constant of aryl amines and hydroxyl aromatic compounds that are sparingly soluble[59].

Flourescence Polarization Method

Fluorescence polarization's fundamental principle. An excitation polarizing filter is used to excite a fluorophore, and the polarized fluorescence is measured using an emission polarizer that is either parallel or perpendicular to the plane of polarization of the exciting light[60].

Mass Pectroscopy

The combination of chromatography and mass spectroscopy allowed for fast determination of constants, which was particularly useful for complicated mixtures[61].

Surface plasma resonance

The use of surface plasma resonance (SPR) to study binding kinetics and strengths is widely acknowledged. SPR is most commonly used to investigate bimolecular interactions. The mechanism of SPR estimation is rather straightforward: a "bait" ligand is bound on the gold surface of the SPR chip[62].

2. **pH Solubility Profile**

It therefore follows the pH max is defined as.

$pHmax = pKa + \log[B]s/[BH+s]$

The aqueous and lipid solubility qualities of a pharmacological material are critical in determining whether it may reach absorption sites, interact with putative therapeutic targets, and eventually be metabolized and excreted. As a result, determining solubility qualities is frequently the first step in preformulation research[63].

3. **Common ion effect**

A common ion significantly reduces the solubility of a moderately soluble electrolyte. The common ion effect suppresses the ionization of a weak acid by introducing an ion that is a result of the equilibrium. The selling out is caused by the complete hydration of other ions, which eliminates water molecules as a solvent. The salting process is reversed in cries with larger anions. Benzoate and saliva, for example, open the water structure. These hydro topics improve the solubility of sufficiently water soluble drugs like diazepam. A frequent solvent interaction that is often overlooked is the common ion effect. When a common ion is added to a moderately soluble electrolyte, its solubility is typically lowered.

Chlortetracycline, methacycline, papaverine, cyproheptadine, bromhexine, and triamterene are examples of antibiotics.

4.Thermal effect

When a mole of solute is dissolved in a huge quantity of solvent, the heat generated or absorbed is referred to as the heat of solution. Most frequently, the solution process is endothermic, or its profile is positive, raising the solution temperature. Increase the solubility of the medication. Variations in solubility are caused by temperature changes. This can be calculated by taking the temperature of the solution, i.e. HS.

lnS = - ΔHS (1)/R + C/T

Where,

dC / dt = dissolution rate, S = molar solubility at temp. T (° K), R = gas constant.

When a mole of solute is dissolved in a huge amount of solvent, the heat emitted or absorbed is referred to as heat of solution. It is calculated using the solubility value of a saturated solution equilibrated at a constant temperature over the desired temperature range. The temperature range should typically include 5°C, 25°C, 37°C, and 50°C. If the heat of the solution is positive (endothermic process), the temperature of the solution will rise. Increased the solubility of the medication. The heat of solution for non-electrolyte and un-ionized weak acid and weak bases dissolved in water ranges from 4 to 8 Kcal/mol[65].

4. **Solubilization**

Restricted experiments should be used to evaluate possible solubilization mechanisms for drug candidates with weak water solubility or insufficient solubility for expected solution dosage forms during preformulation. Co-solvents such as ethanol, propylene, glycol, and glycerin can often improve the solubility of weakly soluble nonelectrolytes by orders of magnitude. The amount of solubilization caused by the drug's chemical structure. That is, the more the solubilization produced by co-solvent addition, the more nonpolar the solute.

Preformulation studies for drug candidates with poor water solubility or insufficient solubility for the intended solution dosage form should involve restricted tests to investigate probable solubilization mechanisms. Some techniques are there for increasing solubility are change in pH, dielectric constant, solubilzation by surfactant, complexation, hydrotropy, chemical modification of drug. Preformulation investigations for a drug candidate with poor water solubility or insufficient solubility for predicted solution dosage forms should involve restricted tests to investigate probable solubilization mechanisms. The addition of a co-solvent to the aqueous solution is a common way of improving solubility. Co-solvents such as ethanol, propylene glycol, and glycerin can often improve the solubility of weakly soluble nonelectrolytes by orders of magnitude[66].

The hydrophobic interactions of water at the nonpolar solute/water interfaces are disrupted by these co-solvents, which solubilize drug molecules. Ethanol, sorbitol, glycerin, and PEG are popular and appropriate co-solvents in the formulation of aqueous liquids for oral solutions. Dimethylacetamide is commonly used in parenteral products. However, owing of the unpleasant odor and taste, its usage in oral liquids is restricted. For dissociated pharmacological compounds, co-solvent effects are usually significantly weaker. Some weakly soluble drugs, such as caffeine, can be solubilized in micellar solutions such as 0.01M Tween 20 or through molecular complexes. During the preformulation step, these exact formulations are usually not developed[67].

Novel technologies

Hot melt method- The simplicity and cost-effectiveness of this technology are its key advantages. it was the first to suggest the melting or fusion method for generating fast-release solid dispersion dosage forms. This procedure involves heating a physical mixture of a drug and a water soluble carrier until the two dissolve. The melted liquid quickly cooled and solidified, resulting in a final solid mass that is crushed, pulverized, and sieved before being compressed into tablets using tableting agents[68].

Solvent evaporation method- To make a solid solution, first dissolve both the medicine and the carrier in a common solvent, then evaporate the solvent under vacuum. This allows them to make a solid solution of the highly lipophilic - carotene in a very water soluble carrier[69].

Hot melt extrusion is similar to fusion with the exception that the extruder causes significant mixing of the components[70].

Nanosuspension technology has been established as a viable option for efficiently delivering hydrophobic medications. This approach is used to treat medicines that are insoluble in both water and oils. A pharmaceutical nanosuspension is a biphasic system composed of nano-sized drug particles stabilized by surfactants and intended for parenteral and pulmonary administration via oral and topical routes. Nanosuspension particles are generally below one micron in size, ranging between 200 and 600nm on average.

Super Critical Fluid (SCF) process

It may effuse like a gas through porous solids, bypassing the mass transfer barriers that hinder liquid flow through similar materials. The ability of SCF to dissolve things such as liquids or solids is far superior than that of gases. Furthermore, around the critical point, minor changes in pressure or temperature cause huge changes in density, allowing many supercritical fluid properties to be "fine-tuned." At near-critical temperatures, SCF are very compressible, allowing minor changes in pressure to significantly alter density and mass. 38 Following the dissolution of the drug particles in the SCF (usually carbon dioxide). They have the potential to re-crystallize at significantly lower particle sizes. The SCF approach micronizes pharmaceutical particles within a narrow range of particle sizes, frequently down to submicron levels[72].

Inclusion complex formation-based technique is a chemical complex in which one chemical component has a cavity into which another chemical compound can fit. Van der Waals bonding is used exclusively in the interaction between both the host and the guest. [2] Inclusion compounds have a broad definition is provided channels generated between molecule in a crystal lattice where guest molecules can fit. Various technical adaptations have been made to prepare inclusion complexes of medicines that are poorly water soluble. Methods include kneading, lyophilization/freeze drying, and microwave irradiation[73].

Hydrotrophy is a solubilization process in which a high amount of a second solute is added to increase the water solubility of another solute, and the compounds used in hydrotropy are known as hydrotropes[74].

6. **Partition coefficient**

The ratio of concentrations of a substance in a combination of two immiscible solvents at equilibrium is known as a partition coefficient (P) or distribution coefficient (D). As a result, this ratio represents a comparison of the solute's solubilities in these two liquids. The partition coefficient describes the concentration ratio of unionized compound species, whereas the distribution coefficient describes the concentration ratio of all compound species[75]. It is given as-

$Po/w=[C_{oil}/C_{water}]$ equilibrium

The concentration of the drug in each layer is determined after shaking it with a mixture of octanol and water.

Log P = un ionized compound) org / (un ionized compound) aq

The partition coefficient, also known as the distribution coefficient, is a ratio that is largely independent of the concentration of dilute solutions of a specific solute species. When logP = 0, the chemical is soluble in both water and solvent. If the log P of a compound is 5, it is 100,000 times more soluble in the partitioning solvent. A log P = −2 indicates that the substance is 100 times more soluble in water than it is in air, indicating that it is very hydrophilic. Lipophilic drugs have partition coefficients greater than 1, whereas hydrophilic drugs have partition coefficients less than 1. Although the partition coefficient appears to be the best predictor of absorption rate, the impact of dissolution rate, pKa, and solubility on absorption should not be ignored. Lipids found in living membranes are complicated and difficult to isolate in their purest form. However, analyzing how a pharmacological molecule distributes itself between water and an immiscible organic solvent can provide an indicator of relative lipid solubility. When a solute is supplied to two immiscible liquids that are in contact, it will distribute itself in a fixed ratio between the two phases. The partition coefficient, also known as the distribution coefficient, is a ratio that is largely independent of the concentration of dilute solutions of a specific solute species. The partition coefficient can be determined using a variety of organic solvents, including chloroform, ether, amyl acetate, isopropylmyristate, carbon tetrachloride, and n -Octanol, with the latter gaining growing acceptance[76].

Method for finding partition coefficient are Shake-flask method, Chromatographic method., Counter current and filter probe method, Tomlinson's filter probe method, Micro electrometric titration method, Automated instrument is now available. fermentation broth.

Shake flask method[77]- or 30 minutes, the medication that has been dissolved in one solvent is shaken with the other partitioning solvent. Allow 5 minutes for the mixture to rest. The aqueous solution is centrifuged, and the drug content is determined. It can be used for a variety of things, including:

- Used to determine the solubility of compounds in both water and mixed solvents.
- It is used to investigate structural activity relationships in drug absorption in vivo in a homologous drug series.
- Partition chromatography can help with phase selection (HPLC), plate selection for TLC, and mobile phase selection (eluents).
- This insight can be put to good use in the extraction of crude drugs.
- Antibiotics can be recovered from fermentation broths, and biotechnology-derived pharmaceuticals can be recovered from bacterial cultures.
- For therapeutic drug monitoring, pharmaceuticals are extracted from biologic fluids.
- Study of the distribution of flavoring oil between the oil and water phases of emulsions and absorption of pharmaceuticals from dosage forms (ointments, supplements, TDDS).

7. **Dissolution**

Drug particle dissolution is influenced by physicochemical parameters such as chemical form, crystal habit, particle size, solubility surface area, and wetting qualities. The modified Noyes- Whiting equation defines the rate at which a pharmaceutical material dissolves with a fixed surface area throughout dissolution[78].

$$Dc/dt=DA/Hv(C_s-C)$$

D is the diffusion coefficient,

h is the diffusion layer thickness at the solid-liquid interface.

Cs is the concentration of a saturated solution of the solute in the dissolution medium at the experimental temperature

A is the surface area of the drug exposed to dissolution media

v is the volume of media

And at time t, C is the drug in solution. Changes in surface, area, surface crystal shape, and interstitial wetting complicate dissolution investigations with drug solutions. Dissolution profiles with extra medication, on the other hand, can be utilized to identify metastable polymorphs or solvates[78]. Types of dissolution apparatus given below in table 3.

There are several elements to consider while designing a dissolution test.

- Dissolution apparatus-related factor.
- Factor that has to do with the dissolving fluid
- Parameter for the process

USP Apparatus	Name
Apparatus 1	Rotating basket
Apparatus 2	Rotating paddle
Apparatus 3	Reciprocating cylinder
Apparatus 4	Flow through cell
Apparatus 5	Paddle overdisc
Apparatus 6	Cylinder
Apparatus 7	Reciprocating disc

TABLE 3 USP Dissolution Apparatus

In many cases, the rate limiting step in the absorption process is dissolving rate in the fluids at the absorption site. This is true for drugs given orally in solid dose forms as tablets, capsules, and suspension, as well as drugs given intramuscularly in the structure of pellets or suspension. There are two main types of dissolution- Intrinsic dissolution and particulate dissolution

Intrinsic dissolution[79]- The Noyes-Nernst equation accurately describes the rate of disintegration of a solid in its own solution:

$$Dc/dt=AD(C_s-C)/hV$$

A = surface area of the dissolving solid

D = diffusion coefficient

C = solute concentration in the bulk medium

h = diffusion layer thickness

V = volume of the dissolution medium

Cs = solute concentration in the diffusion layer

Cs « C and is essentially equal to saturation solubility S during the early stages of dissolution. A constant surface area and volume V can be maintained. Equation simplifies to Equation under these conditions, with constant temperature and agitation.

$$dC / dt = KS$$

Where K =AD/hV = constant

The intrinsic dissolution rate, as described in Equation, is the rate at which a solid chemical dissolves in a given solvent under set hydrodynamic conditions. In a fixed volume of solvent, the intrinsic dissolving rate is usually expressed as mg dissolved x (min-1 cm- Z). This value aids the preformulation scientist in determining if absorption is dissolution rate-limited. It will determine drug dissolution at various surface areas. It is used to investigate the effects of particle size, surface area, and excipient mixing on dissolving. So, if particle size has little effect on dissolution, alternative methods such as surfactant addition will be investigated.

Particulate dissolution[80]- It will determine drug dissolution at various surface areas. It is used to investigate the effects of particle size, surface area, and excipient mixing on dissolving. So, if particle size has little effect on dissolution, alternative methods such as surfactant addition will be investigated.

C. STABILITY ANALYSIS

The first quantitative assessment of a novel drug's chemical stability is done during preformulation stability tests. These inquiries encompass both solution and solid state research. Experiments are conducted in environments that are reflective of the handling. Candidate for medication preparation, storage, and administration. This section focuses on assessing chemical stability, which is critical for preformulation research. Several bulk amounts are created throughout drug development, showing increased yields due to scale-up and process advancements, as well as the potential for crystability. Following the completion of the initial stability tests, one or more issue models implying stability may arise, which can be utilized for limited testing on future bulk amounts or formulations[81].

1. Stability in toxicological formulation

Because toxicological studies are typically conducted early in the drug development process, it's routine to examine a sample of toxicology preparations for stability and homogeneity concerns. It's usually a liquid drug or an aqueous media that's taken orally. all ions, enzymes, and a range of functional groups can all be found in feed, reducing the shelf life of a medicine significantly. Over time, enzyme activity and moisture levels decrease, while feed composition vary by user. Because temperature affects both enzyme activity and absorbed water mobility, it is suggested that this stability study be undertaken at a temperature equivalent to that of a toxicology lab. In addition to chemical stability, the ease of production and temperature ranges of solution and suspension toxicological preparations should be considered. At the same pH and temperature, drug solubility may suggest that only the medication in solution is decomposing[82].

2. **Solution stability**

The capacity of a pharmaceutical dosage form to preserve physical, chemical, pharmacological, and microbiological qualities during storage and use by a patient is known as drug stability. Pharmaceuticals are utilised for therapeutic purposes depending on their efficacy and safety, and they must be stable. The fundamental goal of this stage of preformulation research is to identify the conditions that must be met in order to generate a stable solution. Factors responsible for pH, temperature, light, oxygen, co-solvent, ionic strength. Aqueous Solution for Injection PH 3 comprising ironotecan HCl, phosphate buffer, and WFI was created in a stable manner by dissolving camptothecins without the use of heat during the manufacturing process[83].

Methodology

In many cases, autoclave conditions are used to place the medicine in the additive solution. Both flint and amber vials are used. This will give you information about oxidation susceptibility.

Exposure to light makes you more vulnerable.

Heavy metal susceptibility.

Compatibility with ethanol, glycerine, sucrose, preservatives, and buffers is commonly tested in oral solutions[84].

3. **Solid state stability**

solid-state drug and to identify excipients that are compatible with a formulation. In contrast to the previous solution stability profile, changes in purity and crystalline nature may have a considerable impact on these solid state studies. Solid state reactions are slower and more complicated on average than solution state reactions. Because of the low number of chemical interactions between drug and excipient molecules, and the possibility of several reactions[85].

4. **Drug excipient compatibility studies**

The medicine is in close contact with one or more excipients in the tablet dosage form, which may influence the drug's stability. The formulator can use knowledge about drug-excipient interactions to help them choose the right excipients. For known medications, this information may already exist[86]. The preformulation scientist must generate the necessary information for novel medications or excipients. A new drug's compatibility screening must include two or more excipients from each class. The drug-to-excipient ratio employed in these tests is entirely up to the preformulation scientist's discretion[87].

Importance of drug excipient compatibility[88]

- The dosage form's stability can be improved. Any physical or chemical interaction between the drug and the excipient can have an impact on the medication's bioavailability and stability.
- It aids in the avoidance of unpleasant surprises.
- We can determine the potential reaction by using DECS before formulating the final dosage form.
- It connects the worlds of drug discovery and development. Only a new chemical entity can lead to the discovery of a new medication. After formulation and excipient processing, it becomes a drug product.
- We can identify the appropriate type of excipient with the chemical entities emerging in drug discovery processes utilizing DECS data. DECS data is required for the proposing of an IND (investigational new drug). Before any new formulation can be approved, the USFDA has made it mandatory to submit DECS data.

CHEMICAL CHARACTERISTICS OF PREFORMULATION PARAMETERS

v. **HYDROLYSIS**

Nucleophilic assault of labile groups, such as lactam ester amide imide, is involved. Solvolysis occurs when a solvent other than water is used to destroy the cell. Because there are two interacting species, water and API, it normally follows 2nd order kinetics. Because water is in excess in aqueous solution, the reaction is first order. The presence of hydroxyl ions, hydride ions, divalent ions, and heat, as well as light, ionic hydrolysis, solution polarity and ionic strength, and a high drug concentration, all catalyze the breakdown.

The PH can be adjusted to prevent hydrolysis. Because most powerful medications are weakly acidic or basic in nature. Formulate the drug solution close to its PH of optimum stability, or add a water miscible solvent to the formulation, or use an optimal buffer concentration to suppress ionization, or add a surfactant such as a non-ionic, cationic, or anionic surfactant to stabilize the drug against base catalysis, or reduce the solubility of pharmaceuticals undergoing ester hydrolysis by forming less soluble salts or ester of the drug. Store with desiccants and complexing agents, for example, phosphate ester of Clindamycin[89].

v. OXIDATION

In liquid and solid formulations, this is a highly typical mechanism for drug breakdown. There are two types of oxidation. Auto-oxidation is the first step in the oxidation process. Secondly, The chain reaction of free radicals.

Hemolytic bond fission of a covalent bond produces free radicals when any material reacts with molecular oxygen. Auto-oxidation occurs when these radicals are highly unsaturated and rapidly receive electrons from other substances, resulting in oxidation. Initiation, Propagation, Hydroperoxide Decomposition, and Termination are all steps in the free radical chain process. Oxygen content, light, heavy metals, particularly those with two or more valence states (copper, iron, nickel, cobalt), hydrogen and hydroxyl ions, and temperature are all factors that affect the oxidation process. Because oxidative degradation of drugs occurs in an aqueous solution, the oxygen content can be reduced by boiling water, keeping the formulation in a dark and cool environment, or adding an antioxidant/ reducing agent/chain inhibitors of radical driven breakdown. Antioxidants are classified into two categories based on their solubility. There are two types of soluble oils: oil soluble and water soluble. Water soluble antioxidants, such as hydroquinone, propylgallate, and lecithin, are free radical acceptors and inhibit the free radical chain process, whereas oil soluble antioxidants, such as hydroquinone, propylgallate, and lecithin, are free radical acceptors and inhibit the free radical chain process. Sodium metabisulphate, sodium bisulfate, thioglycolic acid, and thioglycerol, for example, oxidize themselves and prevent the medication from oxidizing[90].

v. REDUCTION

This is a substantially more prevalent drug metabolism mechanism. Hepatic microsomes catalyze a variety of reductive chemical reactions and need NADPH to do so. Cytochrome P-450 catalyzes the reduction of azo and nitro compounds. Alcohol dehydrogenase converts chloral hydrate to its active metabolite trichloroethanol. The active metabolites hydrocortisone is formed when prednisolone and cortisone are reduced. Azo dyes, which are employed as coloring ingredients in pharmaceuticals and food, are broken down by the liver and the intestinal flora to create amines[91].

v. PHOTOLYSIS

Photodecomposition mechanism: The electronic configuration of the medication overlaps with the spectrum of sunshine or any artificial light, causing energy to be absorbed by the electron, which causes excitation. They release the acquired energy and return to the ground state by decomposing the drug because they are unstable. Photosensitization is a phenomenon in which molecules or excipients absorb energy but do not participate directly in the reaction, instead transferring the energy to others who cause cellular harm by triggering radical production. Photosentizer Convert oxygen from its ground state to a singlet excited state, resulting in the formation of superoxide, an anion radical that functions as a potent oxidizing agent[92].

Pathway for photolysis-

- Dipenhydramine, chloroquine, and methotrexate are examples of N-dealkylated drugs.
- Dehalogenation: for example, chlorpropamide and furosemide
- Ca++ channel blockers are dehydrogenated. Naproxen, Flurbiprofen, and Benzoxaprofen are examples of anti-inflammatory medicines that have been decarboxylated.
- Oxidation: In the presence of sunshine, chlorpromazine and other phenothiazines produce n- oxides.
- Noradrenaline, Doxapine isomerization and cyclization
- Rearrangement: Yellow hue of metronidazole and oxidiazine Photodecomposition can be Suitable packaging, antioxidants, medicine protection from light, avoiding sunbathing, photo stabilizers, and coatings all help to prevent this.

v. **POLYMERIZATION**

Artificial neural networks (ANNs) were examined as a preformulation tool for determining physicochemical parameters of amorphous polymers such as hydration characteristics, glass transition temperatures, and rheological properties. This research was conducted using the CAD/Chem neural network simulator, which is based on the delta back-propagation paradigm. Different polymer mixes with established water-uptake characteristics, glass transition temperatures, and viscosity values were used to train the ANNs software.

v. **RACEMIZATION**

The process by which one enantiomer of a molecule, such as a L-amino acid, transforms to the other enantiomer is known as racemization. The complex then switches between the two forms until the ratio of (+) to (–) groups approaches 1:1, at which time it becomes optically inactive. Interconversion between isomers can result in distinct Pharmacokinetic properties (ADME) as well as Pharmacological and toxicological effects. For example, L-epinephrine is 15 to 20 times more active than D-epinephrine, although the activity of racemic combination is just half that of L-epinephrine. It is governed by first-order kinetics. Temperature, solvent, catalyst, and the presence or absence of light are all factors to consider[94].

APPLICATIONS

- In order to produce formulations with the intended efficacy and using cost-effective manufacturing procedures, one needs determine particle shape and size distribution during the preformulation step.
- Good flow characteristics are required for successful dosage form manufacture (tablets and hard gelatin capsules).
- The transfer of powder fill/granules via the hopper of the tableting machine requires appropriate fluidity of materials.
- Preformulation scientists collaborate with analytical departments to produce stability-indicating tests, which are an important part of preformulation testing.
- Because first drug lots may not be pure, a flawless stability-indicating assay may not be accessible in the early stages. However, as the molecule moves through the development stages, purity improves.
- As a result, preformulation experts aim to identify the general circumstances under which the medicine will be stable.
- Levothyroxine sodium, for example, was not stable during its shelf life, and it was discovered after marketing that the cause for lower potency was due to a stability issue with levothyroxine sodium. Because it was sensitive to light, temperature, air, and humidity, it was recalled due to a loss of potency.
- During formulation development, determining solubility during preformulation testing is a critical metric.
- The BCS paradigm can be utilized to develop drug solubility and/or permeability enhancement techniques. Drug absorption rate constants typically vary by only 50 times (0.001 - 0.5 mg/min), although drug solubility can vary

by six orders of magnitude (0.1 g/mL - 100 mg/mL).

- As a result, the formulator has more control over the drug's solubility than its permeability. However, if the dose is really high, this may be problematic. If the medicine is poorly soluble, other formulation options may be tried. In the case of flavopiridol, researchers used HP-b-CD with citric acid to retain the medication solubilized and prevent it from precipitating during injection.

CONCLUSION

Preformulation studies are useful in predicting formulation issues, bioavailability issues, and drug degradation pathways. Preformulation studies provide a clear overview of in vivo drug performance, stability, degradation rate, and shelf life, as well as a mechanism to address these issues. It aids in the selection of the most suitable stable drug candidate by completing HPLC Assay testing, determining partition coefficient, and determining the nature of the drug in the ionic

state. These studies provide us with a direction to achieve our aim. This review article summarizes the findings of the preceding investigations, demonstrating that no pharmacological preparation can be developed without first conducting preformulation trials.

REFERENCES

1. Vilegave K, Gali V, "Preformulation Studies of Pharmaceutical New Drug Molecule and Products; An Overview" .2013; 1(3): 2321-3647.
2. Lachman L, Lieberman Herbert A. and Kanig Joseph L. "The Theory and Pharmaceutical of Industrial Pharmacy". Varghese publishing house, third edition, 171-196.
3. Gopinath R., Naidu R.A.S., "Pharmaceutical Reformulation Studies-Current Review" International Journal of Pharmaceutical and Biological Archives, 2011; 2(5):1391-1400.
4. Albert,A.A. and Serjeant,E.P(1984) ionization constants of Acids and Bases.Wiley,Newyork. 2. Yalkowiski,S.H.andRoseman,T.J(1981).
5. Allen LV, Popovich NG and Ansel H.C:Ansels Pharmaceutical Dosage Forms and Drug Delivery Systems. Lippincott Williams and Wilkins, Wolters kluwer, New York, Edition 9, 2005: 431-492.
6. Bharate SS, Vishwakarma RA. Impact of preformulation on drug development. Expert Opin Drug Deliv. 2013 Sep;10(9):1239-57.
7. Kuehl PJ, Stratton SP, Powell MB, Myrdal PB. Preformulation, formulation, and in vivo efficacy of topically applied apomine. Int J Pharm. 2009 Dec 1;382(1-2):104-10.
8. S. F. Ng , J. J. Rouse , F. D. Sanderson , V. Meidan and G. M. Eccleston , *AAPS PharmSciTech*, 2010, **11** , 1432 —1441.
9. J. I. Wells *Pharmaceutical Preformulation Ellis Horwood (QV744) via Aulton's Pharmaceutics: The Design and Manufacture of Medicines* , M. E. Aulton and K. Taylor, Churchill Livingstone Elsevier, 1998.
10. G. L. Amidon , H. Lennernas , V. P. Shah and J. R. Crison , A theoretical basis for a biopharmaceutical drug classification: The correlation of *in vitro* drug product dissolution and *in vivo* bioavailability, *Pharm. Res.*, 1995, **12** , 413 —420.
11. Trevor M. Jones, CHAPTER 1:Preformulation Studies , in *Pharmaceutical Formulation: The Science and Technology of Dosage Forms*, 2018, pp. 1-41.
12. Deruyver L, Rigaut C, Lambert P, Haut B, Goole J. The importance of pre-formulation studies and of 3D-printed nasal casts in the success of a pharmaceutical product intended for nose-to-brain delivery. Adv Drug Deliv Rev. 2021 Aug;175:113826.
13. Lee CJ, Strachan CJ, Manson PJ, Rades T. Characterization of the bulk properties of pharmaceutical solids using nonlinear optics--a review. J Pharm Pharmacol. 2007 Feb;59(2):241-50.
14. Baghel S, Cathcart H, O'Reilly NJ. Polymeric Amorphous Solid Dispersions: A Review of Amorphization, Crystallization, Stabilization, Solid-State Characterization, and Aqueous Solubilization of Biopharmaceutical Classification System Class II Drugs. J Pharm Sci. 2016 Sep;105(9):2527-2544.

15. Borka, L. Review on crystal polymorphism of substances in the European Pharmacopoeia. Pharm. Acta Helv. 1991, 66, 6–22.
16. Giron, D. Thermal analysis and calorimetric methods in the characterization of polymorphs and solvates. Thermochim. Acta 1995, 248, 1–59.
17. Talaczynska A, Dzitko J, Cielecka-Piontek J. Benefits and Limitations of Polymorphic and Amorphous Forms of Active Pharmaceutical Ingredients. Curr Pharm Des. 2016;22(32):4975-4980.
18. Pudipeddi, M.; Serajuddin, A.T. Trends in solubility of polymorphs. J. Pharm. Sci. 2005, 94, 929–939.
19. Chemburkar, S.R; Bauer, J.; Deming, K.; Spiwek, H.; Patel, K.; Morris, J.; Henry, R.; Spanton, S.; Dziki, W.; Porter, W.; et al. Dealing with the impact of ritonavir polymorphs on the late stages of bulk drug process development. Org. Process Res. Dev. 2000, 4, 413–417.
20. Censi, R.; Rascioni, R.; di Martino, P. Changes in the solid state of anhydrous and hydrated forms of sodium naproxen under different grinding and environmental conditions: Evidence of the formation of new hydrated forms. Eur. J. Pharm. Biopharm. 2015, 92, 192–203.
21. MHD Bashir Alsirawan,Anant Paradkar Impact of the Polymorphic Form of Drugs/NCEs on Preformulation and Formulation Development Book Series:Methods and Principles in Medicinal Chemistry 07 October 2019.
22. Seddon, K.R. Pseudopolymorph: A Polemic. Cryst. Growth Des. 2004, 4.
23. Mura P. Analytical techniques for characterization of cyclodextrin complexes in the solid state: A review. J Pharm Biomed Anal. 2015 Sep 10;113:226-38.
24. Thorn K. A quick guide to light microscopy in cell biology. Mol Biol Cell. 2016;27(2):219-222. doi:10.1091/mbc.E15-02-0088.
25. Gordon RE. Electron microscopy: a brief history and review of current clinical application. Methods Mol Biol. 2014;1180:119-35. doi: 10.1007/978-1-4939-1050-2_7.
26. Franken LE, Boekema EJ, Stuart MCA. Transmission Electron Microscopy as a Tool for the Characterization of Soft Materials: Application and Interpretation. Adv Sci (Weinh). 2017 Jan 31;4(5):1600476.
27. Huang, SC., Pareek, A., Seyyedi, S. et al. Fusion of medical imaging and electronic health records using deep learning: a systematic review and implementation guidelines. npj Digit. Med. 3, 136 (2020).
28. Chiu MH, Prenner EJ. Differential scanning calorimetry: An invaluable tool for a detailed thermodynamic characterization of macromolecules and their interactions. J Pharm Bioallied Sci. 2011;3(1):39-59. doi:10.4103/0975-7406.76463.
29. Nielsen HB. Systematic review of near-infrared spectroscopy determined cerebral oxygenation during non-cardiac surgery. Front Physiol. 2014 Mar 17;5:93.
30. Bunaciu AA, Udriştioiu EG, Aboul-Enein HY. X-ray diffraction: instrumentation and applications. Crit Rev Anal Chem. 2015;45(4):289-99.
31. Koga Daisuke, Kusumi Satoshi, Shibata Masahiro, Watanabe Tsuyoshi Applications of Scanning Electron Microscopy Using Secondary and Backscattered Electron Signals in Neural Structure Frontiers in Neuroanatomy Volume: 15;2021.
32. Bach QV, Chen WH. Pyrolysis characteristics and kinetics of microalgae via thermogravimetric analysis (TGA): A state-of-the-art review. Bioresour Technol. 2017 Dec;246:88-100. doi: 10.1016/j.biortech.2017.06.087.
33. Carr R.L. “evaluating flow properties of solid” Chem.Eng.,1965; 72: 163-168.
34. Sadowski J. And Kubinyi H. “A Scoring Scheme for Discriminating Between Drugs and Nondrugs”. J Med. Chem 1998; 41: 3325–3329.
35. Pathare B, Tambe V, Patel V, “A Review on Various Analytical Methods Used In Determination of Dissociation Constant”, International Journal of Pharmacy and Pharmaceutical Science, 2014; 6(8).
36. Paul K, “Measuring Particle Size Using Modern Laser Diffraction Techniques”, Chem Europe.Com,UK, WR14 1*2.
37. Sanghai B, Aggarwal G, HariKumar SL, Solid self microemulsifying drug deliviry system: a review, Journal of Drug Delivery and Therapeutics. 2013; 3 (3):168-174.

38. Rios, M. Developments in powder flow testing, Pharm. Technol. 2006, 30, 38–49.
39. Shetty N, Cipolla D, Park H, Zhou QT. Physical stability of dry powder inhaler formulations. Expert Opin Drug Deliv. 2020;17(1):77-96. doi:10.1080/17425247.2020.1702643.
40. Vandana KR, Prasanna Raju Y, Harini Chowdary V, Sushma M, Vijay Kumar N. An overview on in situ micronization technique - An emerging novel concept in advanced drug delivery. Saudi Pharm J. 2014;22(4):283-289. doi:10.1016/j.jsps.2013.05.004.
41. Shah RB, Tawakkul MA, Khan MA. Comparative evaluation of flow for pharmaceutical powders and granules. AAPS PharmSciTech. 2008;9(1):250-258. doi:10.1208/s12249-008-9046-8.
42. **K. K. Moravkar, S. D. Korde, B. A. Bhairav, S. B. Shinde, S. V. Kakulade and S. S. Chalikwar** Traditional and Advanced Flow Characterization Techniques: A Platform Review for Development of Solid Dosage Form Indian J Pharm Sci 2020;82(6):945-957
43. Moravkar KK, Ali TM, Pawar JN, Amin PD. Application of moisture activated dry granulation (MADG) process to develop high dose immediate release (IR) formulations. Adv Powder Technol 2017;28(4):1270-80.
44. Rutkowska Ewelina, Pajak Karolina & Jozwiak "Kryzsztof. Lipophilicity- Methods of Determination and Its Role In Medical Chemistry". Aata Polniae Pharmaceutical Drug Research, 2013; 70(1): 3-18.
45. Patel N, "Development and Characterization of Ternary Solid Dispersion Granules of Poorly Water Soluble Drugs: Diflunisal And Mefenamic Acid". Thesis and Dissertations. (2011) Paper 672.
46. Savjani KT, Gajjar AK, Savjani JK. Drug solubility: importance and enhancement techniques. ISRN Pharm. 2012;2012:195727.
47. Murtaza G. Solubility enhancement of simvastatin: a review. Acta Pol Pharm. 2012 Jul-Aug;69(4):581-90.
48. Bou-Chacra, N., Melo, K.J.C., Morales, I.A.C. et al. Evolution of Choice of Solubility and Dissolution Media After Two Decades of Biopharmaceutical Classification System. AAPS J 19, 989–1001 (2017).
49. Reijenga J, van Hoof A, van Loon A, Teunissen B. Development of Methods for the Determination of pKa Values. Anal Chem Insights. 2013;8:53-71. Published 2013 Aug 8. doi:10.4137/ACI.S12304.
50. Manallack DT. The pK(a) Distribution of Drugs: Application to Drug Discovery. Perspect Medicin Chem. 2007;1:25-38. Published 2007 Sep 17.
51. Naji SM, Yusrida D, Kok KP, "Aerodynamic Characterization of Marketed Inhaler Dosage Forms: High Performance Liquid Chromatography Assay Method for the Determination Buclesonide". 2010; 4(12): 878-884
52. Reijega jetse, Hoof van Arno, Loon van Antonie, Teunissen Bram, "Development of Methods of Determination of Pka Values, Analytical Chemistry Insights". 2013; 8: 53-71.
53. Kenny GP, Notley SR, Gagnon D. Direct calorimetry: a brief historical review of its use in the study of human metabolism and thermoregulation. Eur J Appl Physiol. 2017 Sep;117(9):1765-1785.
54. Mäntele W, Deniz E. UV-VIS absorption spectroscopy: Lambert-Beer reloaded. Spectrochim Acta A Mol Biomol Spectrosc. 2017 Feb 15;173:965-968.
55. Fujimoto K, Yang W. Density-fragment interaction approach for quantum-mechanical/molecular-mechanical calculations with application to the excited states of a Mg(2+)-sensitive dye. J Chem Phys. 2008 Aug 7;129(5):054102.
56. Michałowski T, Pilarski B, Asuero AG, Dobkowska A, Wybraniec S. Determination of dissociation parameters of weak acids in different media according to the isohydric method. Talanta. 2011 Oct 30;86:447-51.
57. Xin X, Niu X, Liu W, Wang D. Hybrid Solvation Model with First Solvation Shell for Calculation of Solvation Free Energy. Chemphyschem. 2020 Apr 20;21(8):762-769.
58. Marcano O A, Melikechi N. Continuous wave achromatic thermal lens spectroscopy. Appl Spectrosc. 2007 Jun;61(6):659-64.
59. Noacco N, Rodenak-Kladniew B, de Bravo MG, Castro GR, Islan GA. Simple colorimetric method to determine the in vitro antioxidant activity of different monoterpenes. Anal Biochem. 2018 Aug 15;555:59-66.

60. Hall MD, Yasgar A, Peryea T, et al. Fluorescence polarization assays in high-throughput screening and drug discovery: a review. Methods Appl Fluoresc. 2016;4(2):022001. Published 2016 Apr 28. doi:10.1088/2050-6120/4/2/022001.
61. Urban PL. Quantitative mass spectrometry: an overview. Philos Trans A Math Phys Eng Sci. 2016;374(2079):20150382. doi:10.1098/rsta.2015.0382.
62. Nguyen HH, Park J, Kang S, Kim M. Surface plasmon resonance: a versatile technique for biosensor applications. Sensors (Basel). 2015;15(5):10481-10510. Published 2015 May 5. doi:10.3390/s150510481.
63. Sieger P, Cui Y, Scheuerer S. pH-dependent solubility and permeability profiles: A useful tool for prediction of oral bioavailability. Eur J Pharm Sci. 2017 Jul 15;105:82-90.
64. Li P, Wang S, Samo IA, Zhang X, Wang Z, Wang C, Li Y, Du Y, Zhong Y, Cheng C, Xu W, Liu X, Kuang Y, Lu Z, Sun X. Common-Ion Effect Triggered Highly Sustained Seawater Electrolysis with Additional NaCl Production. Research (Wash D C). 2020 Sep 24;2020:2872141.
65. An J, Lee I, Yi Y. The Thermal Effects of Water Immersion on Health Outcomes: An Integrative Review. Int J Environ Res Public Health. 2019 Apr 10;16(7):1280.
66. Bou-Chacra, N., Melo, K.J.C., Morales, I.A.C. et al. Evolution of Choice of Solubility and Dissolution Media After Two Decades of Biopharmaceutical Classification System. AAPS J 19, 989–1001 (2017). https://doi.org/10.1208/s12248-017-0085-5.
67. Shah DP, Patel B, Shah C, Nanosuspension technology: A innovative slant for drug delivery system and permeability enhancer for poorly water soluble drugs, Journal of Drug Delivery and Therapeutics, 2015; 5(1):10-23.
68. Jana S, Miloslava R. Hot-melt extrusion. Ceska Slov Farm. 2012 Jun;61(3):87-92.
69. McGinity JW, O'Donnell PB. Preparation of microspheres by the solvent evaporation technique. Adv Drug Deliv Rev. 1997 Oct 13;28(1):25-42.
70. Jana S, Miloslava R. Hot-melt extrusion. Ceska Slov Farm. 2012 Jun;61(3):87-92. PMID: 22913823.
71. Patel VR, Agrawal YK. Nanosuspension: An approach to enhance solubility of drugs. J Adv Pharm Technol Res. 2011;2(2):81-87. doi:10.4103/2231-4040.82950.
72. Kankala RK, Xu PY, Chen BQ, Wang SB, Chen AZ. Supercritical fluid (SCF)-assisted fabrication of carrier-free drugs: An eco-friendly welcome to active pharmaceutical ingredients (APIs). Adv Drug Deliv Rev. 2021 Sep;176:113846.
73. Santos CIAV, Ribeiro ACF, Esteso MA. Drug Delivery Systems: Study of Inclusion Complex Formation between Methylxanthines and Cyclodextrins and Their Thermodynamic and Transport Properties. Biomolecules. 2019;9(5):196. Published 2019 May 20. doi:10.3390/biom9050196.
74. Sareen S, Mathew G, Joseph L. Improvement in solubility of poor water-soluble drugs by solid dispersion. Int J Pharm Investig. 2012;2(1):12-17. doi:10.4103/2230-973X.96921.
75. Ulrich, N., Goss, KU. & Ebert, A. Exploring the octanol–water partition coefficient dataset using deep learning techniques and data augmentation. Commun Chem 4, 90 (2021). https://doi.org/10.1038/s42004-021-00528-9.
76. Bannan CC, Calabró G, Kyu DY, Mobley DL. Calculating Partition Coefficients of Small Molecules in Octanol/Water and Cyclohexane/Water. J Chem Theory Comput. 2016;12(8):4015-4024. doi:10.1021/acs.jctc.6b00449.
77. Brusač E, Jeličić ML, Klarić DA, Mornar A. Miniaturized shake-flask HPLC method for determination of distribution coefficient of drugs used in inflammatory bowel diseases. Acta Pharm. 2019 Dec 1;69(4):649-660.
78. Gray, V.A. Power of the Dissolution Test in Distinguishing a Change in Dosage Form Critical Quality Attributes. AAPS PharmSciTech 19, 3328–3332 (2018).
79. Teleki A, Nylander O, Bergström CAS. Intrinsic Dissolution Rate Profiling of Poorly Water-Soluble Compounds in Biorelevant Dissolution Media. Pharmaceutics. 2020 May 28;12(6):493. doi: 10.3390/pharmaceutics12060493.
80. Chu, K.R., Lee, E., Jeong, S.H. et al. Effect of particle size on the dissolution behaviors of poorly water-soluble drugs. Arch. Pharm. Res. 35, 1187–1195 (2012).

81. Ammann C. Stability studies needed to define the handling and transport conditions of sensitive pharmaceutical or biotechnological products. AAPS PharmSciTech. 2011;12(4):1264-1275.
82. Das S, Debnath N, Mitra S, Datta A, Goswami A. Comparative analysis of stability and toxicity profile of three differently capped gold nanoparticles for biomedical usage. Biometals. 2012 Oct;25(5):1009-22.
83. Di L, Kerns EH. Solution stability--plasma, gastrointestinal, bioassay. Curr Drug Metab. 2008 Nov;9(9):860-8.
84. Gomez-Sanchez R, Besley S, Zeliku Z, Young RJ. Method Development and Application of an Accelerated Solution Stability Screen for Drug Discovery. SLAS Discov. 2020 Dec;25(10):1191-1196.
85. Buda V, Baul B, Andor M, Man DE, Ledeţi A, Vlase G, Vlase T, Danciu C, Matusz P, Peter F, Ledeţi I. Solid State Stability and Kinetics of Degradation for Candesartan-Pure Compound and Pharmaceutical Formulation. Pharmaceutics. 2020 Jan 21;12(2):86.
86. Ashizawa K, Uchikawa K, Hattori T, Ishibashi Y, Miyake Y, Sato T. [Solid-state stability and preformulation study of a new parenteral cephalosporin antibiotics (E1040)]. Yakugaku Zasshi. 1990 Mar;110(3):191-201.
87. Chadha R, Bhandari S. Drug-excipient compatibility screening--role of thermoanalytical and spectroscopic techniques. J Pharm Biomed Anal. 2014 Jan;87:82-97.
88. Trevor M. Jones, CHAPTER 1:Preformulation Studies , in *Pharmaceutical Formulation: The Science and Technology of Dosage Forms*, 2018, pp. 1-41.
89. Waterman KC, Adami RC, Alsante KM, Antipas AS, Arenson DR, Carrier R, Hong J, Landis MS, Lombardo F, Shah JC, Shalaev E, Smith SW, Wang H. Hydrolysis in pharmaceutical formulations. Pharm Dev Technol. 2002 May;7(2):113-46.
90. Tingstad J, Dudzinski J. Preformulation studies. II. Stability of drug substances in solid pharmaceutical systems. J Pharm Sci. 1973 Nov;62(11):1856-60.
91. Bharate SS, Vishwakarma RA. Impact of preformulation on drug development. Expert Opin Drug Deliv. 2013 Sep;10(9):1239-57.
92. Janga KY, King T, Ji N, Sarabu S, Shadambikar G, Sawant S, Xu P, Repka MA, Murthy SN. Photostability Issues in Pharmaceutical Dosage Forms and Photostabilization. AAPS PharmSciTech. 2018 Jan;19(1):48-59.
93. Ebube NK, Owusu-Ababio G, Adeyeye CM. Preformulation studies and characterization of the physicochemical properties of amorphous polymers using artificial neural networks. Int J Pharm. 2000 Feb 25;196(1):27-35.
94. Fyhr P, Högström C. A preformulation study on the kinetics of the racemization of ropivacaine hydrochloride. Acta Pharm Suec. 1988;25(3):121-32.

CHAPTER II

TABLETS

Introduction

Powders, pills, cachets, capsules, and tablets are all examples of solid medications that can be taken orally. These dosage formulations are made up of the amount of medication delivered in a single dose They are referred to as a unit and together as even in the case of solid unit dose forms Preparations for long-term action that, contain the technical equivalent of a number of standard medications doses the strict formulation specifications. Tablets Capsules, on the other hand, are currently in use account for more than a third of the total the overall number of drugs and their costs The product is made all around the world. Tablet computers are becoming increasingly popular.

The solid dose form is the most common standard as well as a large number of Compared to other dosage forms, it has a number of advantages. The most common dosing form is tablets. Approximately 70% of all pharmaceuticals are produced in this country. Tablets are used to disperse the medication. Tablets had a variety of shapes and sizes, as well as weight dependent on pharmaceutical medications as well as the proposed administration mode. A tablet is a compacted solid dosage form that contains medications. or without the use of excipients.

Almost majority of the formulations were based on the same idea was applied: lactose monohydrate was used as a diluent, and potato was used as a food. Starch was used as a diluent/disintegrant, while gelatin mucilage was used for granulation. The granulate was dried on trays, sieved, and lubricated with magnesium stearate/talc (1 + 9) as a binder. The majority of these formulations were compressed. On single punch tableting machines and were not well suited to high-speed production. Rotaries. It was common to obtain tablets with inadequate technical qualities. Many At the time, pharmacists made these tablets using their own manufacturing "tricks." There were no direct compression or slow-release pills found. The pharmacopoeia is a collection of pharmacopoeias. Testing for impurities, excellent manufacturing processes, and more than a decade from now, dissolution tests will be conducted. Wet granulation can be done with a number of binders and excipients, but the principles are the same as they were in the past. When starting a new project like designing a generic tablet, it's always good to know what you're up against. excipients used by the generics' originator or other manufacturers This could be the case. In terms of compatibility studies, you'll save a lot of time. Although there are no quantitative data on medicines.org.uk, it is a good place to start.

It's also a good idea to check out the scientific literature on chemical characteristics and functional performance group study of the molecule of the active pharmaceutical ingredient (API) in order to determine, or at the very least be able to predict, various degradation routes Furthermore, the API should have a particle size determination technique. to be created as soon as possible . The ingredients are combined. It could even be impossible to figure out. if the tablet in question is made via direct compression, wet granulation, or dry granulation.

Purified water is desirable if a wet granulation process is chosen. granulation liquid, unless the API is extremely moisture sensitive, hydrophobic, or has unique micromeritic properties. In certain instances, 96 percent ethanol is recommended. 96 percent ethanol / pure ethanol is sometimes used. It's made of water (1 + 1). There are a variety of causes for this, including unknown API physical qualities, unknown excipient physical properties, and unknown production procedures.

Definition

Pharmaceutical tablets are solid, flat, or round, according to the Indian Pharmacopoeia a unit dosage form, biconvex dishes made by compressing a medication or a substance Drugs in a combination, with or without diluents A tablet is a solid dosage form that has been compressed containing a medication or without the use of excipients. They come in various shapes. they are vastly different in terms of size and weight, based on the amount of pharmaceutical ingredients, as well as the desired mode of action administration. [1, 2]

Advantages[1,2,5,6]

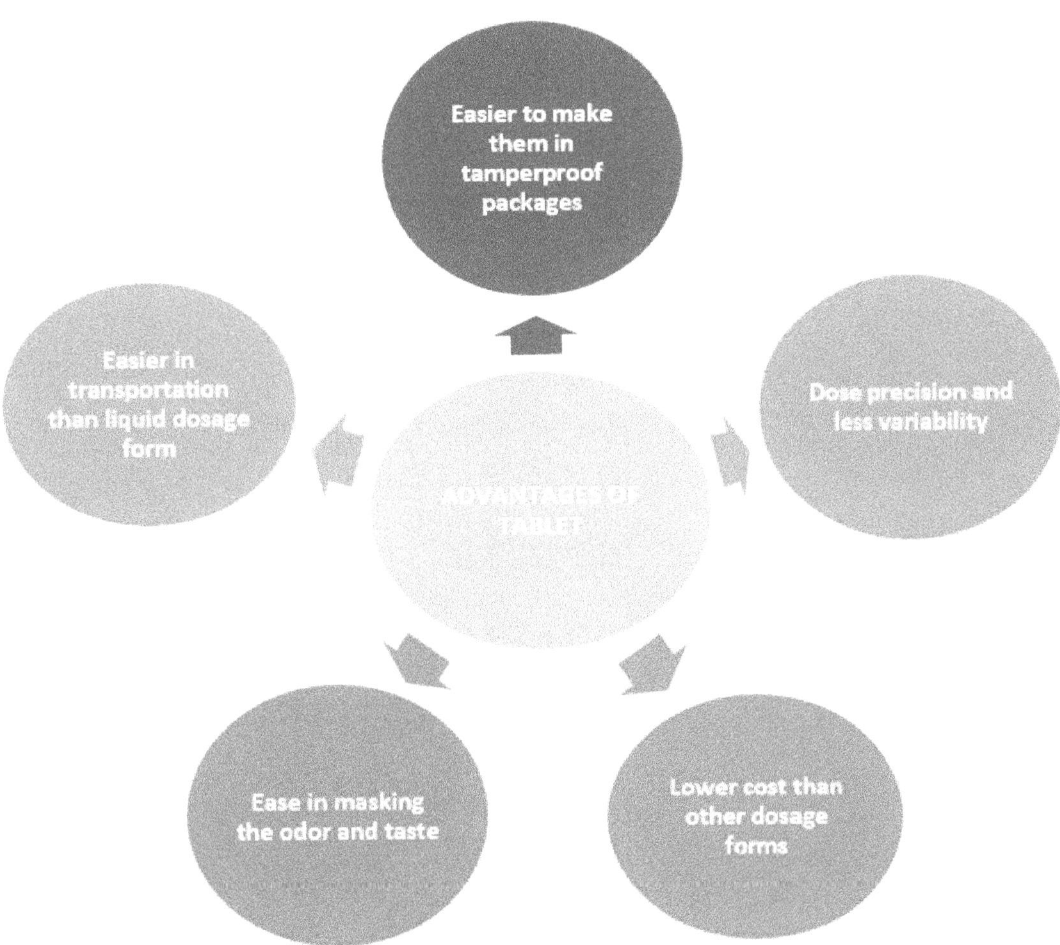

<u>Advantages</u>

<u>Disadvantages</u>[1,2,5,6]

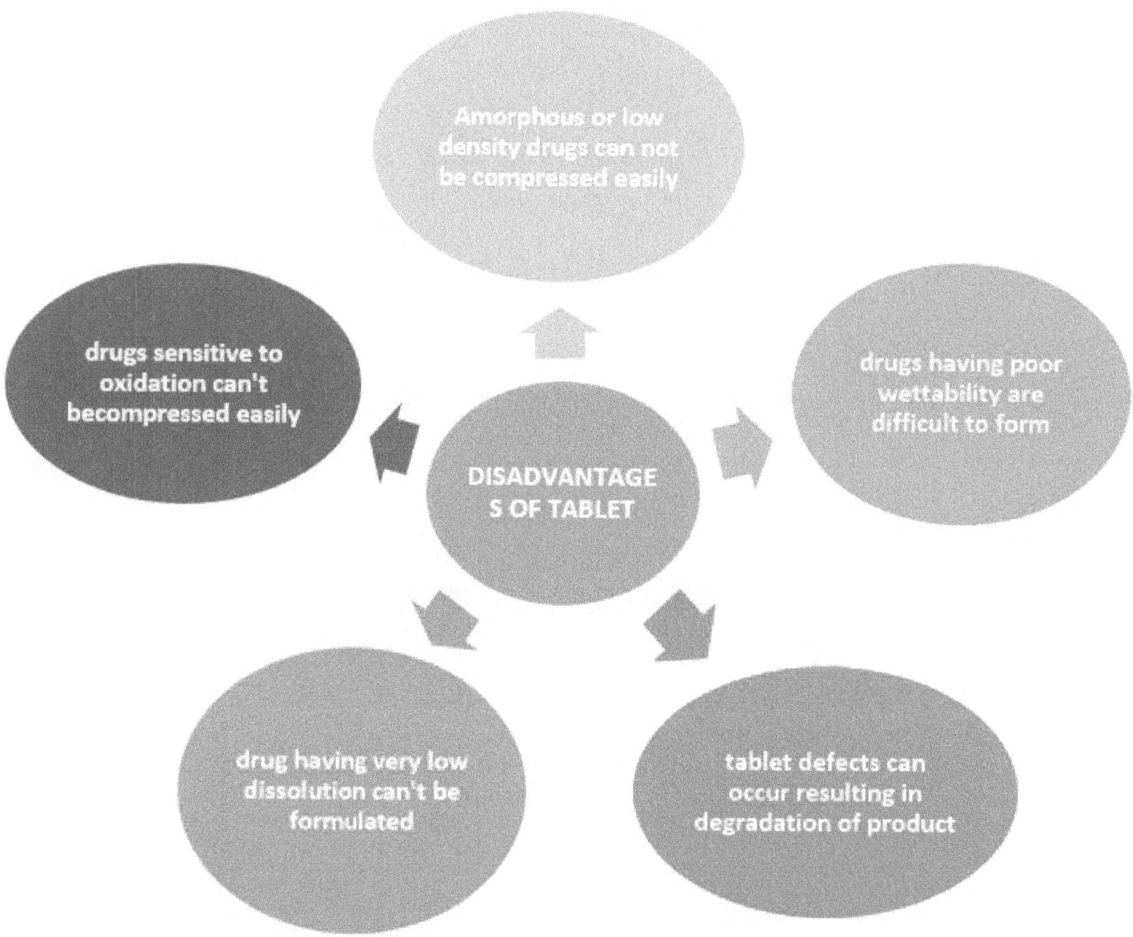

Disadvantages

Ideal characteristics of tablets[5]

1) It should be an elegant product with its own identity that is devoid of flaws such as chips, cracks, and other flaws contamination and discoloration.

2) It should be able to endure the pressure, shocks it has been subjected to while manufacturing, packaging, shipping, distribution and dispensing.

3) Physical stability is essential; it should keep its physical characteristics throughout time

4) The medicament should release in the blood in a predictable and reproducible manner.

5) Chemical stability must be adequate such that no changes may be made over time of the pharmaceutical substance (s).

6) It should be suitable for mass production.

7) It should be easy to swallow and has a low chance of causing a hang-up.

8) Unpleasant odour and unpleasant taste should get masked easily with coating method.

9) A product with sustained or controlled release should be possible with enteric coating.

10) It should be easy to administer and handle.

Classification of tablets

- **Tablets orally used for ingestion**

1.Compressed Tablet (CT)

Compressed tablets are manufactured by compression and have no extra coating in their most basic form. They're constructed of components that are powdered, crystalline, or granular, alone or in conjunction with binders, disintegrants, and controlled-release polymers Lubricants, diluents, and, in many cases, colorants are all used in the manufacturing process.

2.Sugar Coating Tablet (SCT)

Sugar-coated tablets are crushed tablets with a sugar coating. layer of sugar. These coatings can be coloured and are useful in the concealment of pharmacological compounds with unfavourable flavours, unwanted smells, as well as preserving oxidation-sensitive objects.

3.Film Coated tablet (FCT)

Compressed tablets with a thin film coating are known as film-coated tablets. A water-soluble substance layer or film is layered over the tablet. It is possible to use a variety of polymeric compounds with film-forming capabilities. Sugar has the same general qualities as film coating layer with the added benefit of a significantly shorter processing time.

4.Enteric coated Tablet (ECT)

Compressed enteric-coated tablets are coated with chemicals that resist solubility in gastric fluid but dissolve in the stomach and in the small intestine. Tablets containing pharmacological ingredients that have been inactivated or degraded in the stomach can benefit from enteric coating and for individuals who have sensitive mucosa, or it also get used as a means of delaying the onset of symptoms of the medication's release.[7]

5.Multiple compressed tablets (MCT)

Multi-compressed tablets are compressed tablets that have been manufactured by combining the efforts of several layers. There is more than one compression cycle. This method is most effective when stability is required for the active components that need not to be separated. Or if the mixing technique is insufficient to ensure that two or more active components are distributed uniformly.[7]

6.Layered Tablets

Additional tablet layers are created by compressing additional layers of tablet. granulation on top of granulation that has already been compressed. The procedure can be repeated to create two-layered multilayered tablets or perhaps more layers.[7]

7.Press-Coated Tablets

Dry-coated pills are sometimes known as press coated tablets that are made by putting pre-compressed tablets into a machine. Another granulation layer is compressed around the prefabricated tablets using a special tableting equipment. They have all of the benefits of compressed tablets (slotting, monogramming, and so on), while preserving the sugarcoated tablet characteristics of disguising the flavour of the medication component in the most important pills. Manesty Drycota. is an example of a press-coated tablet press.

8.Controlled-Release Tablets (CRT)

Compressed tablets can be designed to release the medicine gradually over a long period of time. As a result, these dosage forms are often known as "prolonged-release" or "sustained-release" dosage forms. These are available in the form of tablets, as well as capsules. There are three different types of versions:

1) Those that release the medicine in response to a physiological situation.

2) Those that release the medicine in a relatively short period of time, such as enteric coatings for example, combine multiple processes to release drug pulses in a constant, regulated manner. These tablets are also known by other names. Extended Release, Sustained Release, and Prolonged Release are some of the terms used. Delayed Release and, if pulsatile pills are used, Repeat Action, Pulsatile Release, or Pulse Release are all terms for the same thing.[8]

- **Tablets for solution (CTS)**

Tablets that are compressed and used for creating solutions or conveying information. Solutions must be labelled with certain features to indicate what they are. They should not be swallowed. Halazone Tablets for Solution and Potassium Permanganate Tablets are two examples of these tablets.[9]

Tablets used in the Oral Cavity

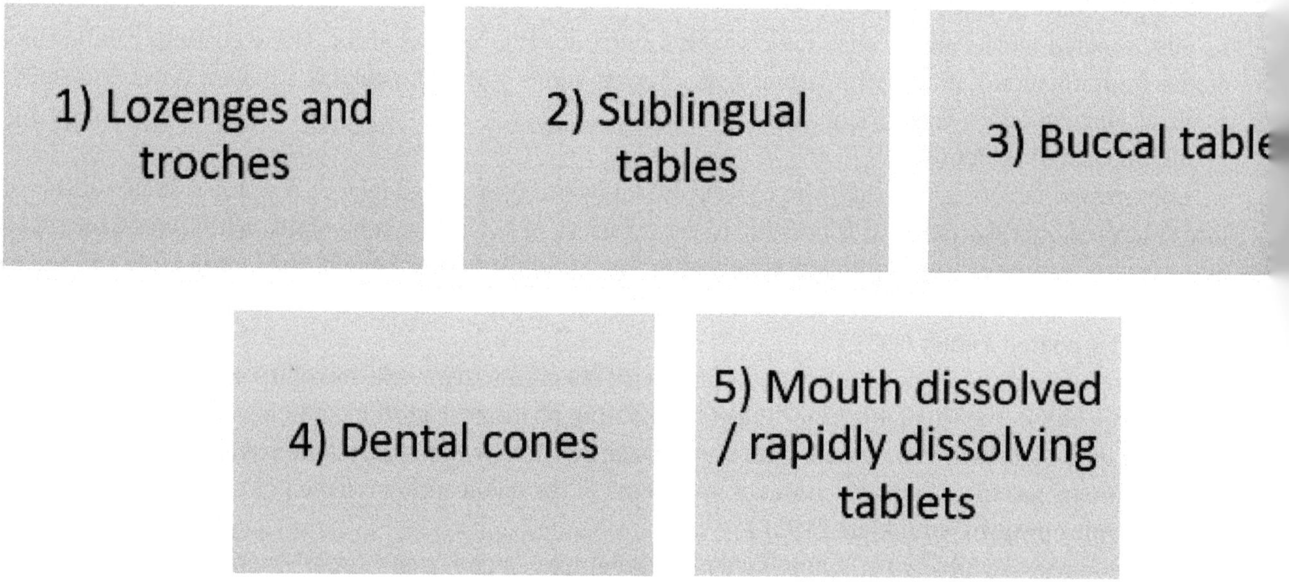

1) Lozenges and troches

2) Sublingual tables

3) Buccal tabl

4) Dental cones

5) Mouth dissolved / rapidly dissolving tablets

- **Buccal and Sublingual Tablets**

Small, flat, oval tablets are used for buccal and sublingual administration. Tabletsmeant to be inserted into the buccal cavity for administrationin some cases, a pouch (the area between the lip and the gum in the mouth) may be present.They are formulated and dissolving or eroding slowly.a tablet that has been compressed to a certain degree of hardness This is how progesterone tablets can be given. Tablets that melt at body temperature are used in other methods. The tablet's grid is:While the medication is in solution, it solidifies. The medication melts once it has melted.is instantly dissolved in water and accessible for absorption,In the absorption of poorly soluble substances, dissolution is no longer a rate-limiting phase. Tablets that are taken under the tongue, such asthose containing nitroglycerin, isoproterenol hydrochloride, or isoproterenol hydrochlorideUnder the tongue, erythrityl tetranitrate is administered. SublingualThe medication ingredients are absorbed quickly once the tablets dissolve.This method of administration allows you to get things done quickly.[10]

- **Tablets used to prepare Solution**

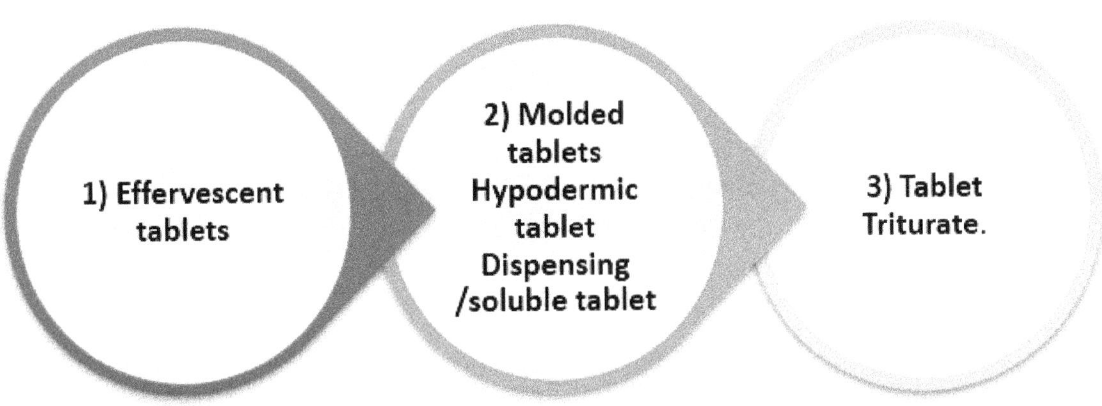

- **Effervescent Tablets**

Effervescent pills contain a pharmacological compound as well as other ingredients. sodium bicarbonate with an organic acid like tartaric or lactic acid. These additives react in the presence of water, releasing carbon dioxide, which acts as a disintegrator and creates effervescence. Except for a few lubricants, there are no lubricants present. Tablets that are effervescent are soluble. Suppositories or inserts that are compressed. Compression is sometimes used to make vaginal suppositories, such as Metronidazole pills. Tablets are commonly used for this purpose. Lactose is used as a diluent. In this instance, as well as in any other, the way in which a tablet intended for administration by means other than swallowing must be indicated on the label. used.[11]

- **Tablets Administered by other Routes**

1. Vaginal tablet

2. Rectal tablet

3. Implants

<u>Excipients used in tablet formulation</u>[6]

Sr.No.	Ingredients	Example
1.	Diluents	Calcium Phosphate: Carboxymethylcellulose Calcium: Cellulose: Dextrin: Lactose: Microcrystalline Cellulose: PR gelatinized Starch: Sorbitol: Starch
2.	Binders	Acacia: Alginic Acid: Carboxymethylcellulose: Cellulose: Dextrin: Gelatin: Liquid Glucose: Magnesium Aluminum Silicate: Maltodextrin: Methylcellulose: Povidone: Sodium Alginate: Starch: Zein
3.	Lubricants	Calcium Stearate: Glyceryl Palmitostearate: Magnesium Oxide: Poloxamer: Polyvinyl Alcohol: Sodium Benzoate: Sodium Lauryl Sulfate: Sodium Stearyl Sulfate: Stearic Acid: Talc: Zinc Stearate
4.	Glidants	Magnesium Trisilicate: Cellulose: Starch: Talc: Tribasic Calcium Phosphate
5.	Anti-adherents	Corn Starch: Metallic Stearate: Talc
6.	Disintegrants	Alginic Acid: Carboxymethylcellulose: Cellulose: Colloidal Silicon Dioxide: Croscarmellose Sodium: Crospovidone: Potassium Polacrilin: Povidone
7.	Coloring agents	FD&C or D&C Dyes or Lake Pigments
8.	Flavoring agents	Ethyl Maltol: Ethyl Vanillin: Menthol: Vanillin
9.	Absorbents	Kaolin: Magnesium Aluminum Silicate: Tricalcium Phosphate

<u>Excipients used in tablet Formulation</u>

Table-1- ingredients used in tablet formulation

- **Diluents:** Diluents are fillers that are used to increase the bulk of a tablet when the drug dosage is insufficient. Also used to boost performance, cohesiveness, allowing direct compression.
- **Binders:** Binders provide cohesiveness when the tablet is compressed directly.
- **Lubricants:** Lubricants are the substance use to prevent adhesiveness between the material of tablet and the machinery parts like dies and punches surfaces and it also helps in reducing friction between the particles, and it may improvise the flow rate of tablet granulation.
- **Glidants:** These are intended to facilitate the granular flow and reduces particle-particle friction.
- **Anti-adherents:** these are the substances added to the tablet to keep the substances devoid of clinging of tablet from the tablet press wall surface.

- **Disintegrants:** When added to a tablet formulation, it makes it easier to break or when it comes into contact with water, it disintegrates.in the GIT repository.
- **Coloring Agents:** Colors are used in a variety of ways. The function of the colours and pigments in a tablet is threefold:

  (A) Drugs that are off-color are masked
  (B) Production Identification
  (C) Production of a more refined and beautiful product

- **Flavoring Agents:** Flavoring oils are a type of flavoring agent. Chewable pills require this ingredient. The oil is added in a dry form, such as Beadlets that have been sprayed dry.
- **Absorbents:** these are the material used with hygroscopic materials. When in tablet formulation, material is hygroscopic, it needs absorbents to absorb the excess water so that the tablet can be punched and formulated.

<u>Granulation Method</u>

There are mainly three method of tablet preparation.

A. Wet granulation method
B. Dry granulation method
C. Direct Compression

Wet granulation method

This method is the most widely used method. It involves several steps including the weighing the materials, granulation, mixing and passed through mesh for screening, damp mass is separated, drying and finally tablet compression. After that, the main active component, diluent, and disintegrant are combined together. Which is followed by passing through the sieve (sifting). The binding agent solutions are combined with the initial mixture and stirred. The quantity of binding agent used in order to, avoid soaking of the tablet should be adequate. If the powder isn't wetted correctly then the grains will be too soft. And can be dismantled during lubrication, which is difficult to achieve during the tablet compression process.

Drying method which is most commonly preferred in the past was the Tray Drying which now replaced by a novel approach namely, Fluid-bed dryers.

After drying, these tablet granules are facilitated to screening, generally of 60-100 mesh size. For meshing, nylon cloth is preferred. And soon after meshing, lubricant is added to provide proper filling in the die.[12]

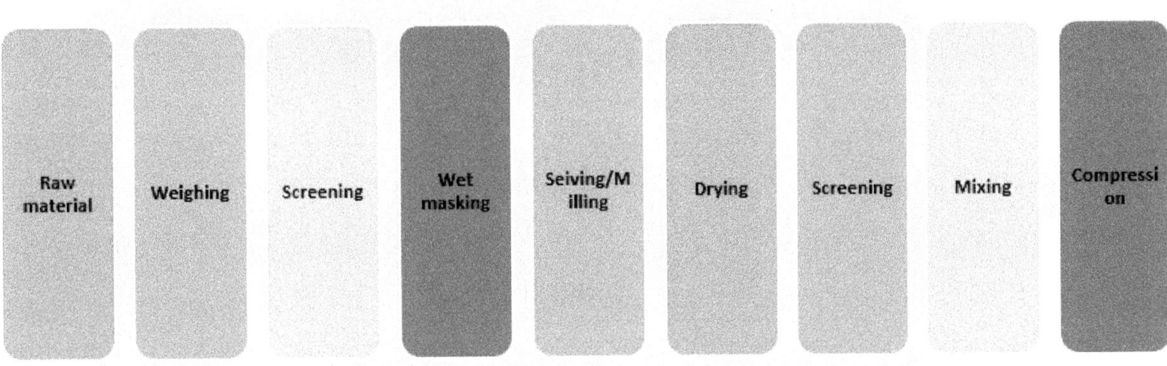

Wet granulation method

Dry Granulation Method

This method is preferred when the ingredients are extremely volatile and sensitive to moisture or can't withstand high temperature during drying. Double compression or Dry granulation usually gets rid of many steps that can cause slugging of the powder mass.

Mainly the ingredients are the active component, Active Pharmaceutical Ingredient (API) along with diluents and lubricants, which are blended together to form slug. Then the slug that is compressed is sent through the mesh and further to mill, and then remaining lubricant is poured in the granules, mixed thoroughly and followed to compression. This is done to facilitate easy compression and sticking is avoided by adding lubricants.[12]

Dry Granulation Method

Direct Compression

As the name suggests, "Direct Compression", it involves Compression of granules directly and form tablet. This method is preferred when the major drug component is the API i.e., 86-90% of total weight. [12,13]

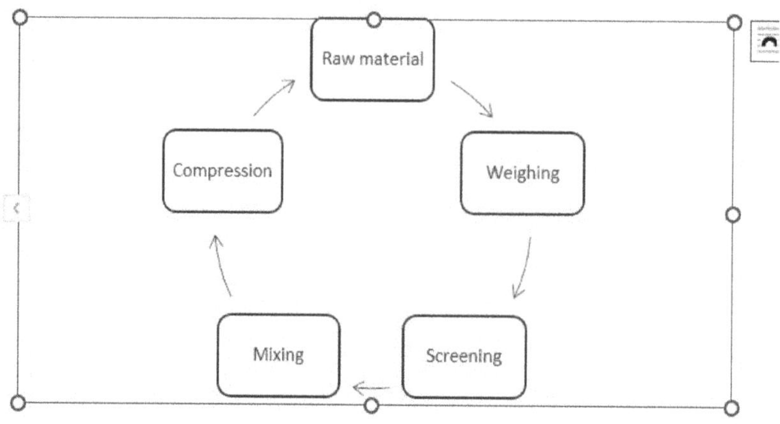

Direct Compression

Figure 3- Direct compression

Compression and Processing Problems[14]

1. **Capping:** Air entrapment in the granular material causes partial or total separation of the top or bottom of the tablet.

2. **Lamination:** Due to air entrapment in the granular material, the tablet is separated into two or more layers.

3. **Cracking:** When deep concave punches are employed, the rapid expansion of tablets causes cracking.

4.**Chipping:** is caused by extremely dry particles.

5. **Sticking:** This refers to the granulation material's attachment to the die wall.

6. **Picking:** This is the process of removing material from the tablet's surface and adhering it to the punch's face.

7. **Binding:** More binder in the granules or moist granules causes this difficulty.

8. **Mottling:** It occurs in colored medicine that is a different colour than the rest of the granular material (excipient-related), poor granular material mixing (process-related), dirt in the granular material or on punch faces, or oil spots caused by the use of an oily lubricant.

9. **Double Impression:** Due to the unrestricted rotation of the punches, which have some engraving on the punch faces, there is a double impression.

TABLET COATING

A tablet is a pharmaceutical solid dosage form made up of a powdered mixture of active ingredients and excipients that has been pressed or compacted into a solid. Tablets are one of the most used dose forms all around the world. Coating is a method of applying an essentially dry outer layer of coating material to the surface of a dosage form in order to obtain specific benefits. Tablets, capsules, multiparticulates, and drug crystals are all examples of oral solid dosage forms that can be coated. When coating composition is applied to a batch of tablets in a coating pan, a sticky polymeric film forms on the tablet surfaces. The applied coating transitions from a sticky liquid to a tacky semisolid, and finally to a nonsticky dry surface pans1 before the tablet surface dries. Coatings are used on the external surface of tablets and on components administered within gelatine capsules in a variety of solid pharmaceutical dosage forms. The drug should be ready for digestion and the tablet should release the medication gradually. The coating technique can be customised to control how quickly the tablet dissolves and where the active medicines are taken into the body following intake. [15]

Tablet coating is a typical pharmaceutical procedure that involves coating a tablet or granule containing active medicinal components with a thin polymer-based film (APIs). Coating solid dosage forms is done for a variety of purposes, the most important of which is to manage release profiles. The amount of coating on the surface of a tablet is crucial to the oral dosage form's effectiveness. Tablets are uniformly coated in horizontal rotating pans, with the coating solution sprayed directly onto the tablet bed's free surface. Taste and odour masking, physical and chemical protection, and protection from the stomach environment are some of the benefits of tablet coating. Sugar coating, film coating, and enteric coating are some of the processes used for tablet coating. The development of coating systems that address the many difficulties associated with solvent-based coatings is a recent trend in pharmaceutical technologies. Coating ingredients are directly coated onto the surface of solid dosage forms without the need of any solvent in these new technologies. Electrostatic dry coating, magnetically assisted impaction coating, compression coating, hot melt coating, powder coating, and supercritical fluid coating are among the solventless coatings available. Recent coating techniques include magnetically assisted impaction coating, electrostatic dry coating in solventless coatings, aqueous film coating, and Supercell coating technology.

TYPES OF COATING[17]

Tablet coating is usually done in one of three ways:

1. SUGAR COATING
2. FILM COATING
3. ENTERIC COATING

SUGAR COATING: The sugar coating process is divided into five steps:

I. Waterproofing/Sealing: creates a moisture barrier while also hardening the tablet surface.

II. Subcoating causes the tablet size to rapidly increase and the tablet edges to round off.

III. Grossing/Smoothing: this step smooths out the subcoated surface and raises the tablet size to the predetermined dimension.

IV. The tablet's colour and final dimensions are determined by colouring.

V. Polishing: Gloss is a feature of polishing. The following are the characteristics of the sugar coating process. [18]

CHARACTERISTICS OF SUGAR COATING- These are shown in table 1

TYPE	CHARACTERISTICS	SUGAR COATING
TABLET	Appearance	Round with high degree of polish
	Weight increase	30-40%
	Logo or break lines	Not possible
PROCESS	Operator training required	Considerable
	Adapatibility to GMP	Difficulty arises
	Process stages	Multiple
	Functional coatings	Not possible

Table : CHARACTERISTICS OF SUGAR COATING

FILM COATING:

i)If all of the following questions are answered affirmatively, then film coating is a viable option: I Is it required to disguise an unpleasant taste, colour, or odour?

ii) Is it necessary to regulate medication distribution?

iii) What size, form, or colour constraints must be imposed on the developmental work for tablets?

Ideal film coating material criteria include:

i. solubility in the coating preparation solvent of choice; and
ii. solubility requirements for the intended usage, such as free water solubility, slow water solubility, or pH-dependent solubility.
iii. Ability to generate a beautiful product
iv. High resistance to heat, light, moisture, air, and the substrate being coated
v. No inherent colour, taste, or odour
vi. High compatibility with other coating solution ingredients
vii. Non-toxic and pharmacologically inactive
viii. High crack resistance
ix. Film former should not cause bridging or filling of the debossed tablet
x. Printing method compatible [19]

MATERIAL USED IN FILM COATING

MATERIAL	TYPES	USES
Film former	Non enteric, enteric	To control the release of drug
Solvents	-	To dissolve or disperse the polymers
Plasticizer	Internal Plasticizing External Plasticizing Internal Plasticizing External Plasticizing Internal, external plasticizing	It Pertains to the chemical modification of the basic polymer that alters the physical properties of the polymer. It incorporated with the primary polymeric film former, changes the flexibility, tensile strength, or adhesion properties of the resulting film It Pertains to the chemical modification of the basic polymer that alters the physical properties of the polymer.
Colorants	Inorganic and natural color	For light shade: concentration of less than 0.01% may be used For dark shade: concentration of more than 2.0% may be required
Opaque extenders	-	Formulations to provide more pastel colours and increase film coverage

MATERIAL USED IN FILM COATING

ENTERIC COATING:

Susceptible/permeable to intestinal fluid. Resistance to gastric fluids. Most coating solution components and the drug substrate are compatible. A continuous film is formed. Nontoxic, inexpensive, and simple to use; ability to be easily printed. [20]

The Following Polymers Are Used For Enteric Coating:

1. Cellulose acetate phthalate (CAP)
2. Acrylate polymers
3. Phthalate of hydroxy propyl methyl cellulose
4. Phthalate of polyvinyl acetate

RECENT TRENDS IN TABLET COATINGS

ELECTROSTATIC DRY COATING

For the first time, electrostatic dry powder coating in a pan coater system was used to develop an electrostatic dry powder coating procedure for tablets. The dry powder coating technique has been developed to create tablets with a smooth surface, good coating consistency, and a release profile that is comparable to that of the tablet cores. This unique electrostatic dry powder coating approach for pharmaceutical items provides an alternative to aqueous or solvent-based coating processes.

MAGNETICALLY ASSISTED IMPACTION COATING

In a magnetically assisted impaction coating (MAIC) device, a technique for calculating coating time is created. The mixture of host, guest, and magnetic particles is supposed to remain in a fluidized state with a Maxwell–Boltzman type velocity distribution. The collisions between the particles are thought to be critical for impinging the guest particles onto the surface of the host particles, generating a semi-permanent coating on the surface of the host particles. The numerical density of host particles, the diameter ratio of host and guest particles, the height of the fluidized particle bed, and the material qualities of the host and guest particles all influence the coating time. The bed height has an optimal value for which the coating time is the shortest.[22]

AQUEOUS FILM COATING TECHNOLOGY

Because the sugar-coating method is time-consuming and dependent on the abilities of the coating operator, it has been phased out in favour of film coating technology. This process began with the use of organic solvents such as methylene chloride, but due to environmental and regulatory concerns, it has now been substituted by aqueous film coating. Furthermore, any organic solvent is far more expensive than purified water. As a result, switching from organic solvent-based coating to aqueous solvent-based coating makes the coating process more cost-effective.

The drawbacks of organic solvent-based film coating systems and the benefits of aqueous-based systems have long been known. Film coating technology has progressed to the point that aqueous coating is now the norm rather than the exception.

SUPERFICIAL COATING TECHNOLOGY

Supercell Coating Technology is a cutting-edge tablet coating that deposits precise amounts of coating ingredients on tablets, even if they are exceedingly hygroscopic or friable. This "conventional" approach of tablet coating often results in a non-homogeneous output due to its inconsistency and imperfection. Edges of tablets can be ground off, intagliations can be filled in with coating material, and edges and corners may not be coated with the same thickness as the tablet faces since the tablets are stacked in huge rotating pans and vented for hot air drying. Furthermore, present technology cannot cover particularly hygroscopic tablets, nor can flat or other irregular shapes be coated reliably. To avoid "twinning," where two or more tablets stay together, this process must be carried out carefully. A Wurster-type coating equipment can also be used to coat tablets, although tablet attrition precludes all but the hardest tablets from being coated this way.

SUPERCELL COATING TECHNOLOGY

SCT, a Niro Pharma Systems technology, successfully tackles all of these issues with a tiny, modular architecture. The continuous small-batch coating method used by SCT is reliable and efficient. The tablets are coated in SCT in batches ranging from 30 to 120 grammes, which scale up linearly to production capabilities. The coating spray is applied to the tablets in the same direction as the drying gas, resulting in a more efficient procedure (Figure 10). The tablets move rapidly and consistently across the spray zone thanks to SCT's innovative air distribution plate design, getting only a tiny quantity of coating every pass and so attaining improved coating accuracy. Because the procedure is shorter, measured in seconds or minutes rather than hours, it is friendlier on the skin. According to Niro Company, traditional tablet coating technologies produce variable and imprecise outcomes, resulting in non-regular results that can impact tablet behaviour. When a small batch of pills is created for clinical trials, this result can introduce a level of unpredictability that becomes more significant. Coating tablets are fed into big rotating pans and vented for hot air drying in traditional coaters, but this can result in tablet edges being ground off, intagliations being filled in with coating material, and edges and corners not being coated to the same thickness as the tablet faces. According to Niro, inconsistencies like this limit the usage of customised release coatings. The SUPERCELLTM Coating Technology can be used to cover friable tablets, as well as flat or very oblong tablet shapes. The drying time is relatively short in this procedure, allowing for the coating of very hygroscopic tablets. Deposition precision is good enough that Active Pharmaceutical Ingredients (APIs) can be placed onto tablets, and uniform layers of flavour masking or modified release coatings can be applied in a single continuous batch.[24]

Quality Control Test [25]

The systematic determination of physical, chemical, mechanical, biological, or microbiological properties of tablets on the basis of in-house (non-pharmacopoeial), pharmacopoeial standards such as BP, USP, Ph. Eur., Ph. Int., JP, IP, ChP, or other guidelines such as ICH is known as tablet quality control testing or tablet evaluation. Quality control tests of tablets or examination of tablet physical, chemical, and bioavailable qualities are required to develop the optimum tablet and thereafter monitor tablet production quality, Bioequivalence vs. Bioavailability. To evaluate tablets or conduct quality control tests on tablets, a variety of approaches are used. All tablet quality control or evaluation tests are divided into three categories:

A. Non-Pharmacopoeial or Non-Official Tests or In-House Tests of Tablet:

1.Appearance/ Description

2.Thickness and Diameter

3.Hardness

4.Organoleptic properties

Non-Pharmacopoeial or Non-Official Tests

B. Pharmacopoeial or Official Tests of Tablets:

1. Identification Tests
2. Friability
3. Disintegration
4. Weight Variation
5. Uniformity of Dosage Unit
6. Dissolution
7. Assay
8. Impurities

C. Specific Pharmacopoeial Tests of Tablets

1.Microbiological Examination of tablets

2.Acid-Neutralizing Capacity

3.Quality test of Splitting Tablets with Functional Scoring

4.Water content

Conclusion

Tablets are most widely preferred dosage form as they are self-administrable and easy to carry and handle. They are the most stable dosage form which doesn't get deteriorated easily with reference to external environment. The formulation of tablets is also an easy process. And with advancement in machinery and technology, modified release tablets are also easily formulated which provide better bioavailability and great patient compliance. Tablets are the dosage form which have great acceptability as it is the most conventional type of dosage form. Alongside, they are inexpensive to manufacture and have certain other advantages like, it can be formulated according to the need of the patients for eg control release, sustain release, enteric coated tablets, etc. To understand each form, these are classified by various different routes and different type of delivery system.

REFERENCES

1) Leon Lachman, Herbert A. Lieberman, Joseph L. Kanig: The theory and Practice of Industrial Pharmacy, Varghese publication house, 3rd edition, 1990, 293-373.

2) Herbert A. Liberman, Martin M. Rieger and Gilbert S. Banker, pharmaceutical dosage forms: Tablets; volume-I.

3) Al-Achi A (2019) Tablets: A Brief Overview. Journal of Pharm Practice and Pharmaceutical Science. 2019(1): 49-52.

4) Nagashree K. Solid dosage forms: Tablets. Research and Reviews: Journal of Pharmaceutical Analysis. 2015.

5) Kaur Harbir. International Research Journal of Pharmacy. 2012, 3 (7).

6) G. Hymavathi, J. Adilakshmi, K. Dwarathi, M. Kavya, G. Pravallika. Review Article on In process Problems and Evaluation Tests of Tablet Manufacturing. International Journal of Research in Pharmaceutical and Nano Sciences. 2012, 3(7).

7) D. M. Jariwala, H. P. Patel, C. T. Desai, S. A. Shah and D. R. Shah. A Review on Multiple Compressed Tablets. Journal of pharmaceutical sciences and boiscientific research. 2016, 6(3). 371-379.

8) Purushottam R. Patil, Vaibhav D. Bobade, Pankaj L. Sawant and Rajendra P. Marathe. Emerging Trends In Compression Coated Tablet Dosage Forms: A Review. International journal of pharmaceutical sciences and research. 2016, 7(3). 930-938.

9) Bhavjit Kaur, Shivani Sharma, Geetika Sharma, Rupinder Saini, Sukhdev Singh, Meenu Nagpal, Upendra K Jain, Mandeep Sharma. A Review of Floating Drug Delivery System. Asian journal of biomedical and Pharmaceutical Sciences. 2013. 3(24) , 1-6.

10) Anita , Anil Singh and Ankit Dabral. A Review On Colon Targeted Drug Delivery System. International journal of pharmaceutical sciences and research. 2019; Vol. 10(1): 47-56.

11) Renu, Jyoti Dahiya, Pawan Jalwal, Balvinder Singh. The Pharma Innovation Journal 2015; 4(5): 100- 105.

12) Nilesh Lahanu Gawade, Raosaheb Sopanrao Shendge. A Review on Chewable Tablet. Journal of Emerging Technologies and Innovative Research (JETIR). March 2020, Volume 7, Issue 3.

CHAPTER III

LIQUID ORALS

INTRODUCTION

The homogeneous liquid preparation containing one or more active substances with or without being dissolved in a medium for oral administration is referred to as liquid oral.

Examples: syrup, linctus, oral drop, emulsion, suspension, solution, etc.

Advantages of liquid orals:

1. Easy to swallow for children as well as elderly patients.
2. More bioavailability than solid.
3. Mask the unpleasant taste by adding an additive (flavoring agent)
4. No need to shake the container in case of solution.
5. By measuring a varied volume, the dose of the pharmacological ingredient can be readily and conveniently altered.
6. In comparison to solid dosage forms such as tablets and capsules, there is more dosing flexibility.

Disadvantages of liquid orals:

1. It's difficult to cover up unpleasant tastes.
2. The contents are at risk of being lost if the container breaks.
3. Bacterial contamination is more likely to occur in liquids
4. In solution, there is less stability.
5. The dose form is bulky and heavy, which creates difficulties with transportation.
6. Some drugs have a low solubility.

SOLUBILITY

Solubility is the greatest amount of solute that can dissolve in a known quantity of solvent at a given temperature.

Factors Affecting Solubility:

1. Temperature:

The solubility of most drugs/additives increases as the temperature rises.

2. Agitation:

It brings fresh solvents into touch with the surface of the solute. Agitation causes the solute to dissolve more quickly. However, only the rate at which a solute dissolves is affected by agitation. It has no control over how much of the solute dissolves. No matter how much the system agitates, an insoluble substance will stay undissolved.

3. Molecular Shape:

The shape of the particles also affects the solubility.

4. Molecular Size:

The molecular weight and size of solute molecules increase as they become larger.

The bigger the particle, the less soluble and vice versa.

5. pH: The majority of the medications are weak acids or bases. In water, they are insoluble or just slightly soluble, although their salts are soluble. The pH of these substances' surroundings has a significant impact on their solubility.

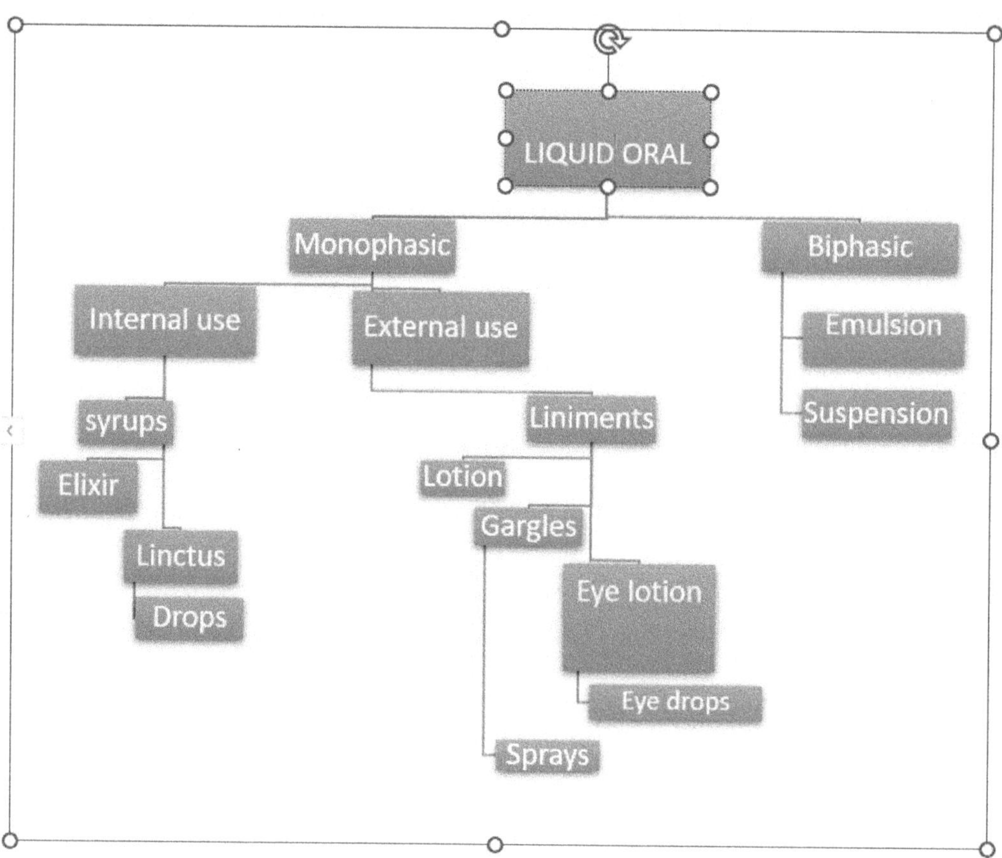

<u>**SYRUPS:**</u>

Syrups are aqueous solutions of sugar (66.7%) or sugar substitutes that contain a flavouring component in a highly concentrated form.

Types of Syrups:

1. **Simple syrup:** It contains 66.7% of sugar.

2. **Medicated syrup:** It contains API (Active Pharmaceutical Ingredient) eg: cough syrup.
3. **Flavored syrup:** It does not contain API (Active Pharmaceutical Ingredient) eg: Raspberry syrup.

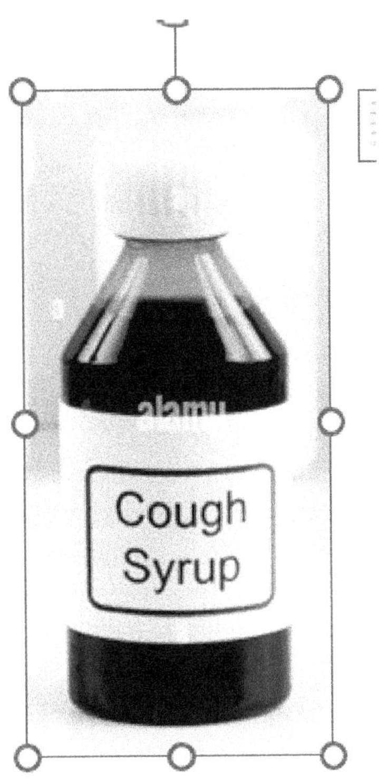

FORMULATION AND MANUFACTURING OF SYRUPS

Additive and Components:

1. Preservatives: must be added to liquid orals to protect them from bacteria. One preservative is not enough for all the formulations. Individual preservatives are to be selected for different formulations.

Examples: sodium benzoate, chlorobutanol, benzalkonium chloride, boric acid.

2. Sweetening Agents: Sweetening agents typically make up a large amount of the solid content in dosage forms that require them.

Examples: sucrose, liquid Glucose, saccharin, aspartame, etc.

3. Viscosity maintaining agents: It's sometimes necessary to enhance the viscosity of a liquid, either to improve palatability or locality.

Example: methylcellulose, carboxymethyl.

4. Buffer: Suitable buffer should be added to maintain the product's pH.

Example: phosphate, citrate, carbonate, etc.

5. Antioxidant: A chemical that guards cells against free radical damage.

Example: Ascorbic acid, lycopene, etc.

6. Flavours: Flavours are used to mask the unpleasant taste.

Example: Menthol

7. Vehicle: A vehicle for a liquid dosage form may be a pharmaceutical solvent, a solution, an emulsion, or a suspension.

8. Solvent: It can be a solution, emulsion, or suspension. May be used as a vehicle for a liquid dosage form.

Examples: water, alcohol, glycerine, etc.

Preparation Process:

-weigh the sucrose in a beaker.

-mix with the purified water.

-Heat a water bath till the solution is obtained.

-Use a filter to remove impurities.

-Makeup to the final volume.

ELIXIRS

Elixirs are defined as transparent, fragrant, sweetened, hydroalcoholic beverages meant to be administered orally.

FORMULATION AND MANUFACTURING OF ELIXIRS

Vehicles used in elixirs are water, alcohol, syrup, sorbitol, and propylene glycol.

Adjuncts are used in elixirs are citric acid(chemical stabilizer) ,methyl paraben (preservative),coal tar(coloring agent) ,raspberry syrup(flavouring agent).

Preparation process:

-Elixirs are made by dissolving two or more liquids with agitation or by combining two or more liquids.

-In their respective solvents, the ingredients are dissolved. Alcohol-soluble ingredients in alcohol, for example, and water-soluble compounds in water.

-By adding the aqueous solution to the alcoholic solution, the alcoholic strength is maintained.

-The combination is then increased in volume to the desired level (q.s.).

-Because the alcoholic strength has been lowered, the product may not be clear at this point due to the separation of some of the flavoring components.

-After allowing the elixir to sit for a while, oil globules begin to form.

-After that, the elixir is filtered.

-To absorb excess oils, talc might be used.

-The result of filtration is a clear product.

EMULSION:

It is defined as the mixture of two immiscible liquids, i.e water, and oil.

Types of Emulsion:

1. w/o: Water in oil emulsion.

2. o/w: Oil in water emulsion.

Emulsifying agent: A compound that improves the stability of an emulsion is known as an emulsifying agent (i.e. Prevention of coalescence and reducing creaming).Examples: agar, pectin, gelatin, tragacanth, etc.

PREPARATION OF EMULSION:

Trituration Method:

It consists of two methods:

i) Dry gum method: The oil is initially triturated with gum and a small amount of water to generate the primary emulsion in this process. The trituration process is repeated until a distinctive 'clicking' sound is heard and a thick white cream forms. After the primary emulsion has been created, the remaining water is gently added to create the final emulsion.

ii) **Wet gum Method:** The gum and water are triturated together to generate a mucilage in this process, as the name suggests. To generate the primary emulsion, the needed amount of oil is gradually added in small proportions while being thoroughly triturated. To make the final emulsion, add the remaining water after the primary emulsion has been generated.

STABILITY OF EMULSION:

DEPENDS ON THE FOLLOWING FACTORS:

1. Cracking: It causes the separation of the phases from each other due to the coalescence of dispersed phase globules.

2. Flocculation: The secondary interaction (Van der Waals' forces) in the flocculated state keeps the droplets separated at a predetermined distance. Shaking the formulation applies shearing force to the droplets, causing them to disperse and form a homogenous formulation. Although flocculation may help to stabilize the formulation, if the interfacial film's mechanical qualities are weakened, droplet coalescence may occur.

3. Creaming: The upward migration of dispersed globules to produce a thick layer at the emulsion's surface is known as creaming.

Stokes law describes the factors that influence creaming:

$$V = 2r^2 (d1 - d2) f/9\eta$$

where,

V = rate of creaming

r = radius of globules

d1 = density of dispersed phase

d2 = density of dispersion medium

g = gravitational constant

η = viscosity of the dispersion medium

4. Phase inversion: The term "phase inversion" refers to the transformation of one type of emulsion into another, for as when the oil in water emulsion transforms into the water in oil emulsion and vice versa.

SUSPENSION:

The term "suspension" refers to a mixture of liquid and solid particles.

FORMULATION AND MANUFACTURING OF SUSPENSIONS:

Wetting agents: They are used to scatter solids in a continuous liquid phase.

Suspending agent: They're mixed in with the medication particles to help them flocculate.

Thickener: To enhance viscosity

Buffers: Buffers are used to maintain pH.

Preservatives: They are used to prevent contamination.

Preparation process:

i) Suspensions are made by blending insoluble components into a smooth paste in a mortar with a vehicle that contains the wetting agent.

ii) To make a slurry, all soluble elements are dissolved in the same portion of the vehicle and combined with the smooth paste in step 1.

iii) The slurry is poured into a graduated cylinder, and the mortar is washed with a part of the vehicle at a time.

iv) Add the vehicle which contains the suspending agent.

FACTORS AFFECTING SUSPENSION:

1. Small particle size: If the particle size is small, then redistribution is easy.

2. Increasing the Viscosity: It is an important parameter for the rate of release of a drug.

3. Temperature: Temperature variation may cause caking.

FILLING METHOD

i. **Gravimetric method:** This approach allows liquid from the bulk liquid tank to flow into containers up to a certain weight limit.
ii. **Volumetric filling:** Positive displacement piston action is used in this method to fill fluids.
iii. **Constant level filling method:** The container is utilized to control the filling of each unit in this procedure. By changing the height to which the container is filled, the fill amount can be changed.

PACKAGING:

The majority of liquid orals come in amber or flint glass vials with plastic or metal lids. When some liquids come into touch with plastic caps, they can cause stress cracking. Metal caps may corrode. As a result, compatible closures must be selected on a case-by-case basis.

EVALUATION OF LIQUID ORAL

i. **Transmittance of light**: A syrup sample is tested for color in a light transmittance meter by passing light through it. The percentage of light transmission as compared to the amount of light available.

Different transmission rates have been established for various grades.

i. **Visual inspection:** For patient adherence and compliance, the physical look of items is crucial, thus it should be as appealing as possible.

- Appearance
- Aesthetic sophistication

iv. **pH measurement:** In quality control testing, measuring and maintaining pH is also critical.

It is done by two methods:

First, simply dip the pH paper and see the numbers written on the paper. And second is a pH meter for high accuracy.

1. **EVALUATION OF ELIXIRS:**

Check the alcohol content:

In most cases, elixirs contain 5-40% of alcohol. less or more content from that leads to eliminating the product.

Viscosity measurement: Viscosity is a characteristic of liquids that is proportional to flow resistance. Viscosity and consistency have a direct relationship with solution stability. If viscosity rises, there's a likelihood that stability will rise as well.

2. **EVALUATION FOR SUSPENSION:**

Sedimentation method:

i. **Sedimentation volume**

$F = Vu/Vo$

Where,

F = sedimentation volume

Vu = ultimate height of sediment

Vo = initial height of the total suspension

ii. Degree of flocculation: It is the ratio between the flocculated suspension's sedimentation volume (F) and the deflocculated suspension's sedimentation volume (F).

$\beta = F/F\infty$

Where,

Floculated sedimentation volume and

Defloculated sedimentation volume

PH measurement: It is done by two methods:

First, simply dip the pH paper and see the numbers written on the paper. And second is a pH meter for high accuracy.

Visual inspection: The physical appearance of items is crucial, thus it should be as appealing as possible.

- Appearance

Micromeritic method: The particle size of the dispersed phase has an impact on suspension stability. The stability of a suspension can be determined by measuring the change in particle size over time.

3. **EVALUATION OF EMULSION:**

Viscosity measurement: Viscosity measurement is used to assess changes that may occur as a result of aging.

Determination of phase separation: Another criterion for evaluating a product is its phase separation. It can be observed visually as well as by measuring the volume of each phase.

Electrophoretic property determination: Electrical charges on surfaces affect flocculation. Factors such as zeta potential are important for determining it. The rate of flocculation is affected by particles.

Electrical conductivity: It is measured with platinum electrodes. w/o will not conduct electricity but o/w will conduct.

4. EVALUATION OF PARENTRALS :

Leaker test: In this test, was used to keep 10-12 bottles on a blotting paper. And after sometimes check the paper if it is wet or dry.

Pyrogen test:

i) LAL test (Limulus monocyte lysate): It is done by the gel-forming ability of Limulus monocyte in the presence of the microorganism.

ii) Rabbit test: it is possible to determine the presence of pyrogen in rabbits by watching a change in body temperature.

Sterility test: This aims to detect the presence or absence of live microorganisms in a sample of containers from a batch of products.

CHAPTER IV

HARD GELATIN CAPSULES

Introduction

Capsules are solid dosage forms meant for oral use where the medicaments or API are covered in a soluble shell. This shell is usually made of gelatin. The patent was granted to Joseph Gérard Dublanc and François Achille Barnabé Mothès, two Frenchmen, for the invention.

Capsules are more advantageous over tablets because of their ability to deliver a variety of forms of mediations like solids, non-aqueous liquids and semisolids as a unit dose solid dosage form. Also, they are neat, smooth and slippery which makes them easy to get swallowed. They are odourless and tasteless which is beneficial for oral administration of drugs having unpleasant odour or taste. They are quite flexible in terms of production. They are made at small scales for clinical studies and at large scale for the purpose of commercial production with the help of machines. Additionally, they undergo immediate drug release. Capsules are not appropriate for administering highly soluble substances like potassium chloride, potassium bromide and ammonium chloride as their rapid release in the stomach may be a cause of gastric irritation. Deliquescent materials tend to absorb moisture from the shell and dry it out leading to extreme brittleness. Use of efflorescent substances can cause softening of capsules as they lose water.

Capsules can be divided into two types, hard gelatin capsules and soft gelatin capsules.

Introduction

Also called as two-piece capsules, hard gelatin capsules consist of two prefabricated parts which are open at one end and close at the other end. The cap is the smaller part which has a slightly larger diameter than the body. The drug is filled in the body and the cap is then inserted. They are different from soft gelatin capsules which are present in one piece and cannot be separated. They can be filled with different forms like pellets, pastes and granules. Hence, they are more versatile as compared to soft gelatin capsules.

Production of Hard Gelatin Capsule Shells

While preparing capsules, we need to verify that the dosage is accurate, stable, consistent, has good bioavailability. Uniform mixing of components is very crucial to avoid drastic therapeutic consequences. Unlike tablet production, capsule production does not costly and lengthy operations like sieving, granulation, or repeated mixing.

Tablets	Capsules
1) weighing	1) weighing
2) preparing ingredients	2) preparing ingredients
3) mixing	3) mixing
4) granulating	4) filling into capsules
5) drying	5) packing
6) sieving	
7)additionof lubricants/mixing/sieving, as necessary	
8) compression	
9) packing	

Table- Operations in the production of tablets vs. capsules

Gelatin shell needs the following raw materials

1. Gelatin: Capsule comprises primarily of gelatin. It is translucent, colourless, flavourless substance derived from collagen present in the animal body. Collagen is irreversibly hydrolysed to gelatin. Mixture of bone and pork skin gelatin is normally used due to its relatively high strength.

   Gelatin is the material of choice as it has the following properties:

- Forms a homogeneous, strong and flexible film.
- Gets readily solubilised in the body fluids at optimum temperature.
- Accepted worldwide in food stuff owing to its non-toxicity.

Gelatin is of two types. Type A is derived from acid treated precursor. Its isoelectronic point exists in the region of pH 9. Type B is derived from alkaline treated precursor whose isoelectronic point exists in the region of pH 4.7. The shell is mostly made up of a combination of both the types though in some cases either one of them can also be used.

1. Colourants: They have mostly two types, water soluble dyes and insoluble pigments. They can be applied to combination. Pigments used are titanium dioxide which is white and imparts opacity to the shell and oxides of iron which are black, red and yellow in colour. Colourants are blended with the gelatin solution during manufacturing process.
2. Plasticizers: They are added to maintain the plasticity of the shell. Glycerol is the most used plasticizer alone with additional ingredients like sorbitol, acacia, sucrose and propylene glycol.
3. Preservatives: they are added to prevent microbial contamination during manufacturing. The moisture content in the final capsules is such that microbial growth is not supported. Antifungal agents are also added. Frequently used preservatives include methyl parabens and potassium bisulphite.
4. Flavouring agents: The use of these is masking the bitter taste of the medicament at a concentration of maximum 2%. E.g., ethyl vanillin, essential oils.
5. Sweetening agents: They impart a sweet taste to the drugs additionally to flavouring agents E.g., Sugar not more than 5%.
6. Diluents: They are used to achieve the desired bulk of the medicament which are generally present in small quantity. It depends on the dose and capsule size. Some examples are lactose, sorbitol and starch.
7. Glidants: They are used to enhance the flow properties of the drug powder for easy filling in the capsules. Various glidants used are talc and magnesium stearate.
8. Absorbents: They are inert materials which act as protective agents for physically incompatible medicaments. Oxides and carbonates of calcium and magnesium and kaolin pose as good adsorbents.

Steps for Manufacture of Hard Gelatin Capsules:

1. Dipping: Pins made of stainless steel are lubricated and dipped into the gelatin solution to form caps and bodies simultaneously. Pins are maintained 228° C temperature and the dipping solution at about 508° C.
2. Spinning: Pins are elevated and rotated two and a half times until they are facing upwards so the solution gets evenly spread on the pin and avoid bead formation at capsule ends.
3. Drying: Large volumes of air is passed through the pins while they are put into an arrangement of hot air ovens. Care must be taken as very high temperature may melt the shell. Over drying can make the shell brittle whereas under drying can make it moist and sticky.
4. Stripping: Capsule shells are stripped off the pins with the help of bronze jaws.
5. Trimming and joining: Capsule cap and body are trimmed using stationary knives corresponding to the desired length. Then they are aligned in channels in a concentric arrangement and joined together. They are then ejected out from the machine.

6. Polishing: Capsules undergo polishing with the Acela Cota pan. Then they are dusted with a cloth and undergo brushing.
7. Sorting: They are passed under conveyor belt to be examined by inspectors to check defects.

Size of capsules

Hard gelatin capsules exist in sizes ranging from 000 (largest) to 5 (smallest). Manual filling machines having capacities 36, 96, 100, and 144 capsules are used.

Figure- Relative sizes of hard gelatin capsules for human use Src. Capsules-I, Industrial Pharmacy-I by Dr. K.L. Senthilkumar, Dr. Atishkumar Shrikisan Mundada, Dr. Rani S. Kankate, Thakur Publication pvt. ltd., pg 115

Size	Volume (ml)	Calculated fill weight (g) at powder density of 0.8 g/cm
000	1.37	1.096
00	0.95	0.760
0	0.68	0.544
1	0.50	0.400
2	0.37	0.296
3	0.30	0.240
4	0.21	0.168
5	0.13	0.104

Table- Volume and capacities of 8 sizes of capsules

Filing, Finishing and Special Techniques for Formulation of Hard Gelatin Capsules

Filing involves the following operations:

1. Rectification: One capsule is passed through the channel at a time to grip the cap end. The capsule is rotated about the cap using a blade. Empty capsules are aligned with their body end facing is downwards.
2. Separation of caps from bodies: The capsule is introduced into a split bushing ring where body is pulled down into the lower portion due to application of vacuum. Owing to its large diameter, the cap does not follow the body in the lower region. Thus, the body is now exposed for filling.
3. Dosing of fill material: The material can be filled in the capsules by various methods

- Auger fill principle
- Vibratory fill principle
- Piston tamp principle

Some manufacturers of capsule filing equipment include Eli Lilly Company, Farmatic SNC, Perry Industries, Park-Davis and Company out of which, the maximum equipment are supplied by Eli Lilly and Park-Davis

4. Replacement of caps and ejection of filled

capsules: The cap is joined with the body. Body is pushed up towards the cap with the help of pins after which the capsule is pushed out of the bushing. Compressed air is also used for this operation.

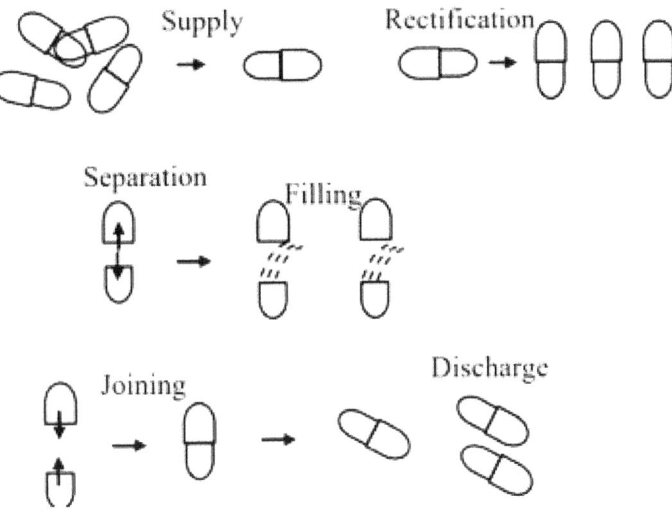

Figure- Capsule filling process Src. Capsules-I, Industrial Pharmacy-I by Dr. K.L. Senthilkumar, Dr. Atishkumar Shrikisan Mundada, Dr. Rani S. Kankate, Thakur Publication pvt. ltd., pg 119

Finished capsules may have powder blend stuck to them. This needs to be removed before releasing in the market. This can be done by dusting or polishing with cleaning wipes in small scale industries. Large scale industries employ the following methods:

1. Pan polishing: Accela-Cota tablet coating pan is used in this process. A polyurethane or cheese cloth acts as a liner to trap the removed dust.
2. Cloth Dusting: A cloth is used for rubbing the capsules which may or may not be wetted with inert oil. This makes the capsule surface glossy.
3. Brushing: Capsules are inserted into the equipment and the soft rotating brushes remove the dust which is permanently removed by the application of vacuum.

Special techniques for formulation are:

1. Imprinting: It is done to provide information on the capsules for identification. Imprinting of empty capsules is preferred to prevent damage, contamination, or poor print quality. Many colours of water or solvent soluble edible ink are used for imprinting.
2. Special purpose capsules: They are treated to decrease their solubility. This delays the absorption of API. For example, formalin treatment of gelatin capsules lowers the solubility. This happens because of the cross linking of gelatin with aldehyde. Also, coating of substances like salol, cellulose acetate phthalate and certain resins modify solubility characteristics.
3. Materials which may react with each other are incorporated in a two-phase system in the capsule. One may include small pellets, tablets, pill, smaller soft or hard capsule. The other may normally be filled in the capsule in the form of powder or granules
4. Nowadays, automatic and semiautomatic machines ae use for the filling of the hard gelatin capsules. They were earlier filled with oils, pill masses etc. Now they also include liquids and semi solid which are filled after melting at ambient temperature

Thixotropic mixtures are filled by increasing sheer. Upon decrease of shear, the viscosity increases which prevents leakage.

Manufacturing Defects

As seen earlier, manufacturing process involves various operations like spinning, stripping, drying, dipping etc. There is always a possibility of formation of defects while passing through these stages.

1. Deliquescent or hygroscopic powder: These substances may absorb the moisture from the shell leading to brittleness and cracking. This can be prevented by adding absorbent.
2. Segregation and homogeneity: Sometimes the particles of the mixture may get segregated due to vibrations of the heavy-duty machines. This is prevented by using particles having invariable particle size and density.
3. Incompatibility: This is common between the different ingredients incorporated in the formulation or with the shell. The physical and chemical properties of the substances used are thoroughly studied before starting with the manufacturing process. Absorbents are inert substances which act as protective agents for physically incompatible medicaments.
4. Improper powder flow during mixing: This may cause non uniformity in the formulation. It can be overcome by adding glidants or lubricants as they enhance the flow properties of powder mixture.
5. Certain substances liquify or form a paste when mixed due to lowering of their melting point. To prevent this, each ingredient is mixed with absorbent separately before mixing them together. They can also be mixed to form a eutectic mixture. Afterwards, the absorbent can be added.
6. Loss of cap or misalignment of cap and body bush: This issue might emerge due to high vacuum during manufacturing. This can be prevented by making sure the right amount of vacuum is applied.
7. Dents or pinholes: Over filling of capsules, incorrect pin size, excess pressure during closing and improper storage conditions can cause these defects. It should be ensured that correct disc size is used, and the dose quantity is accurate.
8. Cracks in capsules: It results from improper storage conditions which results in transferring of moisture from capsule shell to the inner components. Misalignment of cap and body can also be a cause of this problem. Storage conditions need to be checked regularly and a proper setting station should be made.
9. Capsule doesn't get separated: Causes can be incorrect vacuum pump, leakage through filters, improper cap and body alignment. Thus, vacuum pump must have proper capacity. If the vacuum drops below the required level, filters should be check and replaced or repaired if damaged.
10. Inaccurate weight of capsule: This defect arises when the product has poor flow, there is slug formation or incorrect capsule size. Physical parameters, like tapped density, moisture content and particle size distribution

must be checked.

In Process and Final Product Quality Control Tests for Capsules

The pharmacopoeia has provided a list of tests for examining the standard of capsules. IPQC tests include tests for evaluating the physical charecters of capsules whereas quality control tests include assay, mass uniformity, mass variation, dissolution test, disintegration test among others.

IPQC and FPQC tests

1. **Appearance:** Capsule must have uniform appearance. Unrefined changes like hardening, softening, swelling, cracking and discolouration suggests physical instability. Such capsules must be discarded.
2. **Size and shape:** Hard gelatin capsules are cylindrical with sizes ranging from 000 (largest) to 5 (smallest). Soft gelatin capsules exist in a variety of shapes like ovoid, cylindrical, spherical, tubes etc.
3. **Unique identification markings:** They are imprinted on the capsules for easy identification
4. **Assay:** These tests are conducted for the quantitative and qualitative analysis of the Active Pharmaceutical Ingredient (API).
5. **Content of active ingredients:** Individual monographs and calculates of IP are referred for the tests to check the content of API in the capsules. For this assay, not less than 20 capsules are needed. In case 20 capsules are unavailable, not less than 5 capsules are used.

Weight of API in each Capsule (gm)	Subtract from Lower Limit for samples of					Add the Upper Limit for Samples of				
0.12 or less	15	1	10	1	5	15	1	10	1	5
More than 012 but less than 0.3	0.2	1	0.7	1	1.5	0.3	1	0.8	1	1.8
0.3 or more	0.2	1	0.5	1	1.2	0.3	1	06	1	1.5

Table- IP limits for active ingredients

6. **Content uniformity test:** the assay is conducted for about 10 capsules.

The Acceptance Value (AV) for this test is calculated by:

AV= M – X + KS

Where, M = Reference value. X = Mean of individual content (x1, x2...., xn) expressed as percentage of the label claim. K = Acceptability constant. S = Sample standard deviation

9 of 10 capsules should be in the range of 15% (85 - 115%). 10th capsule is beyond ± 15% range, the 20 capsules are assayed. All capsules within range of ± 25% (75 - 125%).

7. **Uniformity of mass:** The contents of a pre weighed container are emptied. The empty shell is weighed and difference in the weight of the filled and empty capsule is taken. This gives us the weight of medicament inside the capsule. This is repeated with 19 capsules and their average is taken.

Average Mass (mg)	Percentage Deviation (%)
Less than 300	10
300 or more	7.5

Table- IP, BP, PhEur Limits for Mass Uniformity

Not more than 2 capsules should deviate from the data given in the table and none of the capsules should deviate by more than twice the percentage given.

8. **Mass variation test:** 10 capsules are individually weighed. Their contents are removed and the capsules ae weighed again. Weight of constituents is the difference in the two weights taken and hence the API content is calculated.

Acceptance Value (AV) is obtained by using:
Xi = Wi × A/W Capsules - I

Where, x1, x2...., xn = Individual estimated contents of the dosage units tested. w1, w2,..., wn = Individual masses of the dosage units tested. W = Mean of individual weights (w1, w2,....., wn).

Maximum limit of AV of 10 capsules is 15%. In case the AV is higher than 15%, the test is repeated with the next 20 capsules and their AV is calculated. To meet the acceptance criteria, the final AV of 30 capsules should be maximum up to 15% and no individual content of the capsule should be less than (1 – 25 × 0.01) M or more than (1 + 25 × 0.0 1) M in calculation of acceptance value.

9. **Disintegration test:** According to B.P., one capsule is introduced to each test tube and the apparatus is suspended in a beaker with 60 ml water at 37 C. If hard capsules float on water surface, then disc may be added. The apparatus is operated for 30 minutes and then the assembly is removed. The capsules pass the test, if no residue remains on the screen of apparatus.

10. **Dissolution test:** For this test, BP or USP dissolution apparatus is used. It consists of a cylindrical glass vessel with a hemispherical bottom, a motor, a metallic drive shaft, and a cylindrical basket. The vessel is immersed in the water bath partially and which also has a heating jacket to maintain temperature inside the vessel at 37±0.5°C. A single capsule is placed in the apparatus, and air bubbles escape from its surface. At definite time intervals, specimens are withdrawn from a midway zone between dissolution medium surface and the top of the rotating basket or blade, minimum 1cm from the vessel wall.

S1	**6**	**Each unit is not less than Q+5%**
S2	6	Average of 12 units (S1+S2) is equal to or greater than Q, and no unit is less than Q-15%.
S3	12	Average of 24 units (S1+S2+S3) is equal to or greater than Q, not more than 2 units are less than Q- 15%, and no unit is less than Q-25%.

Table- BP, USP, PhEur, PhInt and JP Acceptance Criteria for Capsule Dissolution Test

The capsules are continuously tested for 3 stages until the test results confirm at either S1 or S2. The quantity (Q) presents the definite quantity of dissolved API. The 5%, 15%, and 25% values in the capsule are percentages of the labelled content.

11. **Moisture permeation test:** The degree of moisture permeation is necessary containers is crucial for capsule packing. The dosage unit is packed with a colour revealing desiccant pellet. It is then exposed to known humidity conditions and observed for colour change in the desiccant pellet. Absorption of moisture is indicated by colour change.

References

1. *Lachman and Leiberman, Theory and Practice of Industrial Pharmacy, 3rd ed, Varghese Publishing House, Dadar, Mumbai, India*
2. *Dr. K.L. Senthilkumar, Dr. Atishkumar Shrikisan Mundala and Dr. Rani S. Kankate, Industrial Pharmacy-I, 2019, Thakur Publication pvt. ltd., Lucknow, India*
3. *Dr. B. Prakash, Rao S. Rajarajan, Dr. Beny Baby, A Textbook of Industrial Pharmacy-I, 2019, Nirali Prakashan Publication, Pune, India*
4. *Akash Mali, A Brief overview on Capsule, 2015*
5. *Dr. Sven Stegemann, Capsugel, Bornem, Hard gelatin capsules today – and tomorrow, 2nd edition 2002*
6. *Harishchandra Chavan, Chhabra Gurmeet, Gujarathi Nayan, Jadhav Anil, Comparative Study of In-Process and Finished Products Quality Control Test for Tablet and Capsules According to Pharmacopoeias*
7. *S.W. Hoag, Developing Solid Oral Dosage Forms: Pharmaceutical Theory and Practice, 2017, Elsevier*

CHAPTER V

SOFT GELATIN CAPSULES

Introduction

A solid capsule (outer shell) enclosing a liquid or semi-solid center is referred to as a soft gel or soft gelatin capsule (inner fill). Both the inside fill and the outside shell may include active ingredients. Soft gelatin capsules are made of gelatin that has been mixed with glycerin or another polyhydric alcohol, such sorbitol. Preservatives like methylparaben and/or propylparaben may be added to soft gelatin capsules, which have a higher moisture content than hard gelatin capsules, in order to slow the growth of microorganisms. Similar to capsules, they are an oral dose form for medication.

- Soft gelatin capsules are thicker than hard gelatin capsules and need extra substances like glycerin to have a soft texture.
- The thickness, elasticity, and level of residual moisture of the capsule can be altered depending on the formula.
- In the stomach, soft gels dissolve in 20 to 30 minutes.
- The shell will absorb water when it comes into contact with water, begin to fill, and eventually dissolve completely.
- They are ideal for delivering oil-based compositions.
- Because soft gelatin capsules are simple to use and swallow, many consumers prefer them.

Why gelatin is used ?

- Gelatin, which meaning "stiff," is a whitish, dry powder.
- Gelatin is the perfect component for soft gels since it dissolves in the human body at body temperature. The soft gels' gelatin allows for simple ingesting for consumers while safeguarding the active ingredients inside the capsule from oxygen, light, moisture, and dust.

Types of soft gelatin

a. **Chewable soft gels** that release the medication liquid fill matrix when the shell is chewed.
b. **Suckable soft gels** made of a liquid matrix and a gelatin shell carrying the flavouring to be sucked (or just air inside the capsule).
c. **Twist-off soft gels** are those with a tag that can be twisted or cut off to gain access to the fill material.
d. **Soft gels that melt** when used as suppositories or pessaries.

Hard Capsules　　Soft Capsules

Difference between Hard Gelatin and Soft Gelatin Capsules

NATURE OF SHELL

Gelatin, a plasticizer, substances that give the desired appearance (colourants and/or opacifiers), and occasionally flavors make up soft gelatin. Each product's formulation of the capsules' contents is produced specifically to meet its specifications and intended uses.

- GELATIN : Gelatin is the perfect material for encapsulating pharmaceutical compounds because to its unique chemical, physical, and physiological characteristics. The capsule manufacturer has additional requirements, but the gelatin is USP grade. The remaining requirements speak to the gelatins' viscosity, Bloom strength, and iron content.

- BLOOM STRENGTH Bloom strength, which is inversely correlated with gelatin's molecular weight, is a measure of the cohesive strength of the cross-linking that occurs between gelatin molecules. Additionally, it is often referred to as gelatin's gel rigidity or gel strength. By weighing the amount of weight needed to move a plastic plunger in grammes, bloom strength can be calculated (0.5 inches diameter). 17 days were spent with 4 mm at 10°C. It might be between 150 and 250. The resulting capsule shell is more physically stable the greater the gelatin's bloom strength is employed.
- VISCOSITY: The gelatin film's production features are determined by its viscosity, which measures the length of the molecular chain. Gelatin's viscosity was assessed using a 6(2/3) percent concentration of the protein in water at 60°C. Gelatin has a viscosity that can range from 25 to 45 milipoise. When encasing hygroscopic objects or solids, low-viscosity (25 to 32 milli poise), high-bloom (180 to 250 g) gelatins are employed.

- IRON: is always present in raw gelatin, and the amount of iron it contains typically varies depending on how much iron is available in the enormous amounts of water needed to make gelatin. Soft gelatin capsules should not include more than 15 ppm of this element in the gelatins used in their production.
- **PLASTICIZERS:** To ensure mechanical stability, or the elasticity of the capsule shells during and after the drying process, the production of a soft capsule necessitates the inclusion of a non-volatile plasticizer in addition to water. Among plasticizers, glycerol and sorbitol are the most popular. The most widely used soft gelatin capsule plasticizer, glycerol, combines the benefits of a high plasticizer effectivity, sufficient compatibility, and moderate volatility with the capacity to specifically interact with the gelatin, enabling the creation of a stable thermoreversible gel network. Water is the more efficient plasticizer, while sorbitol acts primarily as a moisturizing agent. The strength of the shell is determined by the weight-based ratio of dry plasticizer to dry gelatin (P/G).
- **WATER**: As a solvent, demineralized water is employed. Depending on the viscosity of the gelatin being used, the weight ratio of water to dry gelatin might range from 0.7 to 1.3 (water) to 1.0 (dry gelatin). It typically makes up 30 to 40 percent of the wet gel formulation, and its inclusion is crucial to ensuring correct processing both during the manufacture of the gel and the encapsulation of soft gelatin. Because soft gelatin capsules will either become too soft and fuse together during harsh storage circumstances, or too rigid and brittle, the quantity of water is crucial for optimum physical stability.
- **Colorants/Opacifiers:** To give the shells the desired color and gloss, as well as to allow the shell to shield the fill from light and hide the fill's unappealing appearance, coloring and opacifying agents are routinely utilized. It was decided that the capsule shell's color would be darker than the fill's color. Before choosing a color, mixes should be examined to make sure that storage will not cause the capsule shells to fade or darken due to reactions between the coloring agent and other shell or filling components. When the fill formulation is a suspension, an opacifier, often titanium dioxide, may be added to create an opaque shell or stop light-sensitive fill material from photodegrading. When titanium dioxide is used alone, it produces a white opaque shell, and when it is combined,

it produces a colorful opaque shell.

- **Flavoring Agent**: It is allowed to be used in concentrations of no more than 2%. Examples include ethyl vanillin and essential oils.
- **Sweetening Agent**: These substances, like sugar, can only be used in concentrations of up to 5%.
- **Preservatives:** When gelatin is dry, it is stable. Gelatin is only susceptible to microbe attack in the presence of moisture. Preservatives are necessary as a result. Methyl paraben, propyl paraben, sodium met bisulphite, potassium bisulphate, etc. are a few examples.

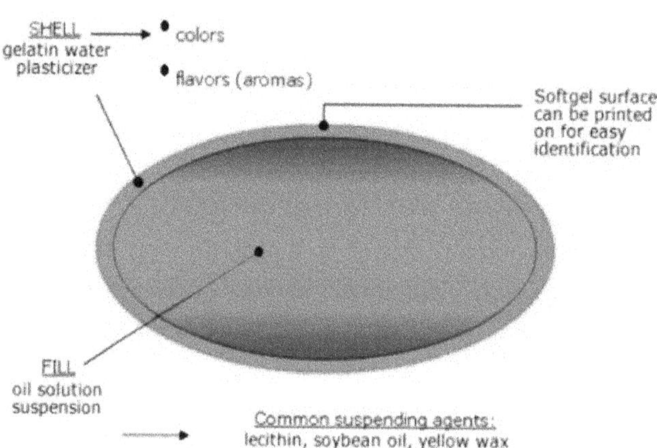

Figure: Anatomy of soft gelatin

NATURE OF CAPSULE CONTENT

- When gelatin is dry, it is stable. Gelatin is only susceptible to microbe attack in the presence of moisture. Preservatives are necessary as a result. Methyl paraben, propyl paraben, sodium met bisulphite, potassium bisulphate, etc. are a few examples.
- The pH range for the encapsulation preparations should be 2.5 to 7.5. Basic treatments can tan the gelatin and influence its solubility, while acidic substances can cause hydrolysis and the leakage of the gelatin shell.
- Liquids that are water-miscible and volatile cannot make up a significant portion of a capsule's composition.
- Solids are put into soft capsules either as a solution or a suspension. The answer is simple to condense. Solids that are insoluble in the solvent system are suspended in capsules.

SIZE OF CAPSULES

Soft gelatin capsules are available in the following shapes and sizes:-

Oblong Soft gel Size: These kinds of soft gel capsules are rectangular or elliptical in shape with one long end. This particular form of capsule has only right angles. It has a fill weight of about 1000 mg and a 20-minimum size capsule.

Round Soft gel Standard Shapes and Sizes: These soft gel capsules are made up of a curving line that completely encloses an area. From the centre of the capsules, the line is equally distant from each point along its length. There are various sizes and colors of these teardrop-shaped capsules.

Oval Soft gel Capsule Sizes: This particular soft gel capsule has a circle-like form, but one end is wider than the other. It has an egg-like appearance. Depending on the density of the enclosed substance, the capsule can store different volumes of the liquid matrix.

Tube Soft gel Sizes : This particular Soft gel capsule is rounded with a flat bottom. The density of the capsule shell determines the distinct colors and sizes of the tube soft gel.

Suppository Soft gel Standard Shapes and Sizes : This type of Soft gel capsule is a bullet whose supply in the market is limited to acceptability by the user. In the earlier days, the capsule was mostly used in rectal and vaginal drug deliver. Furthermore, the current suppository Soft gel capsules are produced in such a way that they have integrated ingredients of active pharmaceuticals.

Twist-off Softgel Capsules Sizes: With this kind of soft gel capsule, the dose for topical and oral applications can be measured. This kind of Soft gel capsule is used to supply the majority of pharmaceutical industries' grade chemicals that are briefly mixed. The majority of twist-off Soft gel capsules are made from carrageenan and seaweed.

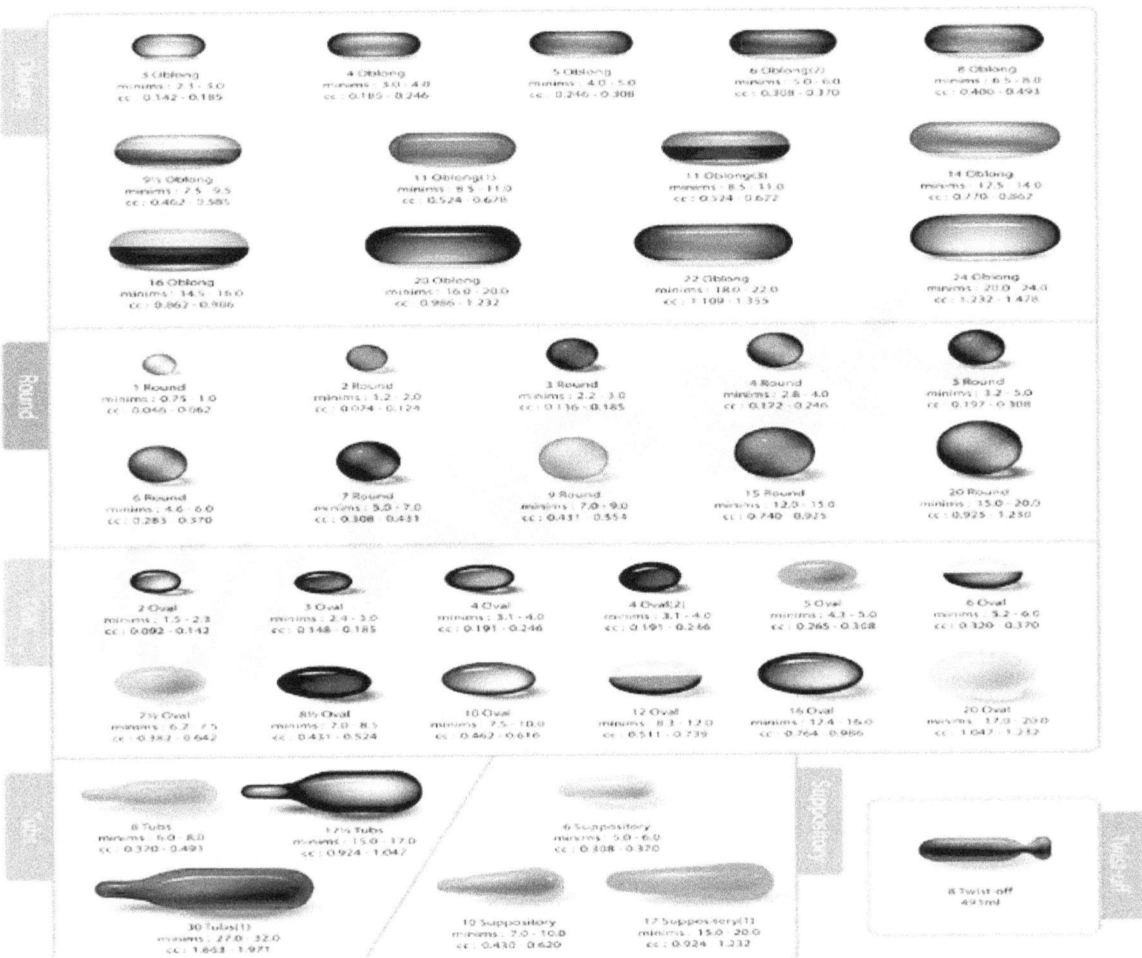

Fgure: Types of soft gelatin capsules.

IMPORTANCE OF BASE ADSORPTION

- Adsorption is defined as the adherence of a solid to a liquid. Base adsorption of solid in liquid bases is required for the filling of suspension of solid in soft gels.
- Base adsorption is calculated as the amount of liquid base in grams needed to make one grams of solids into a capsulatable combination.
- It depends on the particle size and form of the solid, its physical state (crystalline, fibrous, or amorphous), its density, its moisture content, and whether it is hydrophilic or oleophilic.
- The solid(s) must be completely covered in the liquid base in order to determine base adsorption.

PROCEDURE :

- Take two 150 ml beakers.

- Beaker A holds the solid medication (40g), whereas Beaker B holds the liquid base (100g).
- Using a spatula, add a little amount of liquid base to the solid.
- Stirred properly until the liquid base is evenly absorbed by the solid.
- The mixture will have a soft, ointment-like consistency.
- Add liquid base in continuous motion.
- Record the amount of liquid base that was added when the mixture started to thicken and stop flowing.
- As a result, base adsorption has the following formula:

Base adsorption = weight of liquid base / weight of solid

- Lower base adsorption of the solid will result in a larger mixture density and a smaller capsule.

MINIM/GRAM FACTORS

To calculate the solid's "minim per grams" factor (M/g), the base adsorption is utilized (s). The minim per grammes factor is the volume in minims occupied by one gramme of the solid plus the weight of liquid base (BA) necessary to make a capsulatable mixture. It is calculated by dividing the weight of base plus the gramme of solid (BA + S) by the weight of mixture (W) per cubic centimeter or 16.23 minims (V).

:

Minim per gram (M/G) =(BA+S)×V/W

Where,

- M/g factor is mostly utilized in the creation of vitamins.
- BA is used to calculate the solid's minim per gramme factor.
- M/G is the volume in minima filled by one gramme of solid base and the weight of liquid base needed to create a combination that can be swallowed.

BA and M/g Factors of Some of the Typical Solids

Ingredients	Base	BA	M/g
Acetaminophen	Vegetable oil	0.76	25.97
Ascorbic acid	Polysorbate 80	1.10	26.92
Lactose	Vegetable oil	0.75	23.87

PRODUCTION

These techniques are used to make soft gels:

1. Plate process
2. Rotary die process
3. Reciprocating die process
4. Accogel process
5. Seamless process

Plate process:

The manufacturing of soft gelatin capsules utilises this method, which is the oldest commercial procedure. This procedure involves covering a die plate with several depressions, moulds, or die pockets with a warmed sheet of plain or colourful plasticized gelatin. Vacuum is applied to create capsule wells by drawing the sheet into these crannies or pockets. Following that, a liquid containing the drug is poured into the capsule wells. After the filled wells are covered with a second sheet of gelatin, the top plate of the mould is carefully positioned on top. To shape, seal, and cut the capsules into individual units, pressure is then applied to the combined plate. Use of this technique results in soft gelatin capsules that are prepared on a small scale and typically have one flat side.

This approach is not beneficial because the capsules used are too wet and flimsy to endure certain climatic conditions. This apparatus is no longer readily available.

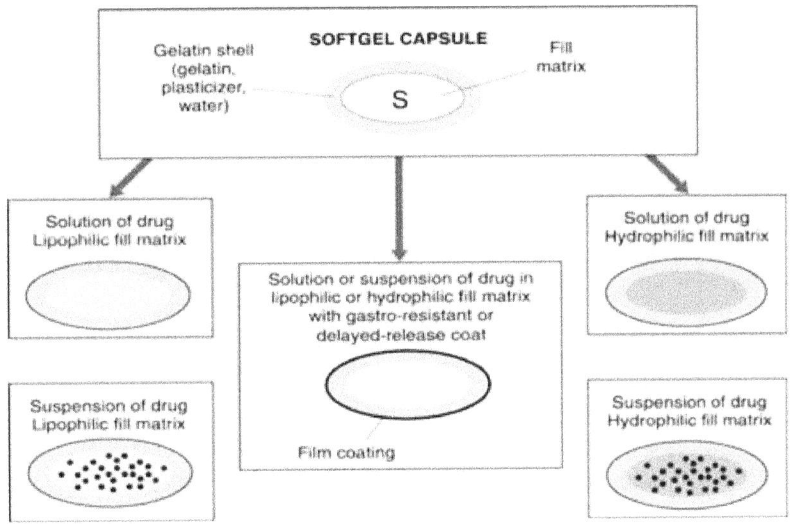

Figure: Plate process of soft gelatin capsules.

Rotary Die Process: In this method, soft gels are continuously created, filled, and sealed. In this technique, liquid gelatin enters the machine as two continuous ribbons from an overhead tank. Between two revolving dies, these ribbons combine to create a gelatin ribbon pocket. Then, using a pump stroke, the precise amount of medication or material is pumped into it. Gelatin pockets that are filled with material are sealed by pressure and heat. To get rid of the mineral oil lubricant, the produced capsules are completely cleaned (naphtha washed). It is then properly dried. The capsules are dried in a tumble-drying tunnel using a lot of pressured air and at a high temperature. The capsules are placed on trays after being moved from the drying tunnel.

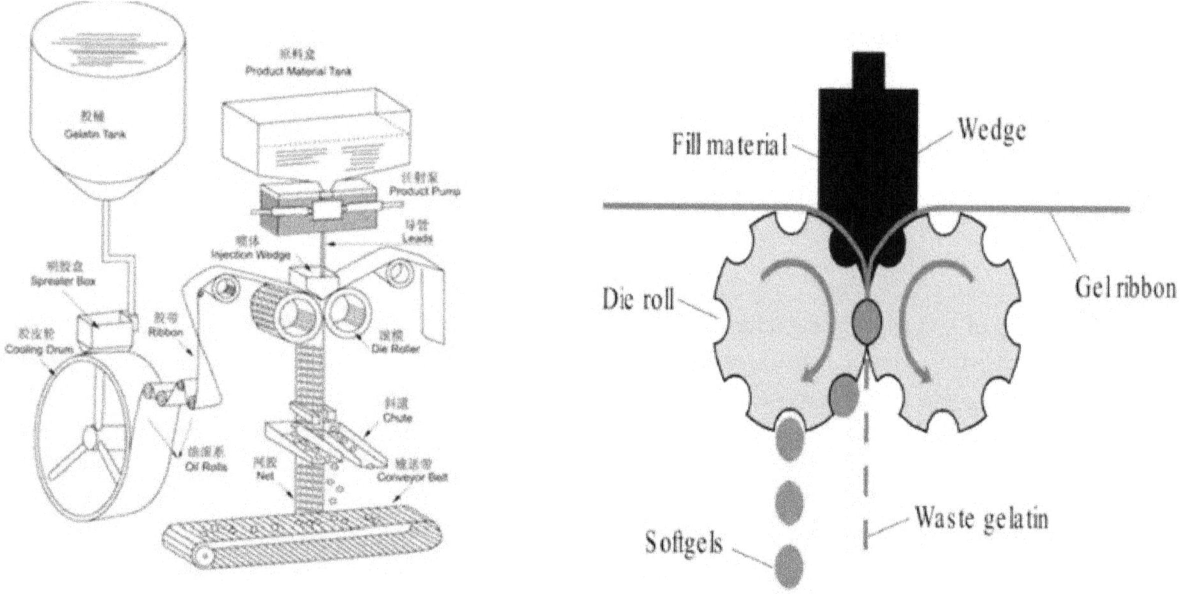

Figure: Soft gel formation mechanism (rotary die mechanism)

Reciprocating Die Process (Norton Capsule Machine):

The Norton Company created this continuous soft gelatin capsule production method in 1949. This method resembles the rotary method in that gelatin ribbons are created and then utilized to encase the fill, but it differs from it in the manner of encapsulation. In order to create rows of pockets in the gelatin ribbons, the gelatin ribbons are fed between a set of vertical dies that open and close continuously. These pockets move through the machinery while being filled with the drug, sealed, formed, and cut out of the film. Following their separation from the ribbons, the capsules drop into a cooled solvent bath, which prevents them from sticking to one another.

Accogel Process:

Although the rotary die method and reciprocating die process could create soft gelatin capsules with pastes and oily liquids inside, Lederle Laboratories created the accogel process in 1949. This continuous process creates soft gelatin capsules with powders and granules inside.

The procedure uses a measurement wheel that revolves immediately above the elasticized sheet of the gelatin ribbon while holding the fill formulation in its cavities under vacuum. Vacuum draws the ribbon into the capsule cavities of the capsule die roll. The fill material is dispensed by the measurement rollers into the gelatin cavities on the die roll that are formed like capsules. The revolving sealing roll, which is coated with another layer of elasticized gelatin, is where the die roll will eventually meet. The created capsules are sealed and sliced by pressure produced by the convergence of two rotating rolls.

Seamless process (Bubble Method):

Without the use of dies, the seamless process creates one-piece soft gelatin capsules. The procedure yields pearls, which are flawless, spherical soft gelatin capsules. It is frequently referred to as a bubble method. In this procedure, the medicinal liquid formulation is distributed via the inner orifice by means of a precision metering pump as a stream of molten gelatin runs through the outer nozzle of a concentric tube at a consistent rate. A pulsing mechanism divides the emerging stream into an irregular but consistent flow of uniform-sized droplets, which results in the creation of droplets encased in molten gelatin. The created capsules are swiftly taken out of the nozzle, allowed to gently solidify, and then automatically expelled from the apparatus.

In Process And Final Product Quality Control Tests

Different pharmaceutical product quality control factors can guarantee the products' optimal therapeutic efficacy, bioavailability, and quality.

1. **Appearance**: The capsule's look should be consistent. There should be a visual or electronic inspection.

2.**Assay:** By employing an appropriate analytical technique, this is carried out to know the existence of an active component.

3. **Content of Active Ingredients**:The range for the active constituent content specified in the monograph, as per Indian Pharmacopoeia. The assay typically uses 20 capsules, or any other quantity that may be specified in the monograph. A reduced quantity, which must not be less than 5, may be used in the event that 20 capsules cannot be procured. The restrictions may be loosened in these circumstances to the extent stated.

When the indicated limitations are between 90 and 110 percent, the criteria of apply. It is recommended to provide proportionately smaller or bigger allowances for limits outside of the range of 90 to 110 percent.

4. **Content Uniformity Test**: British Pharmacopoeia states that 10 capsules (either hard or soft) should be taken at random and tested. Nine tablets out of ten should contain no less than 85% of the labelled medication content and no more than 115%. Not less than 75% and not more than 125% of the active ingredient can be found in the tenth tablet.

5.**Uniformity of weight**: weighed each of the 20 whole capsules. The capsule for the firm gelatin capsule was opened, and the contents were extracted as fully as feasible. If the capsule is made of soft gelatin, take out the contents and wash the shell with a suitable solvent before letting it air dry. The weight of each capsule is determined by weighing the dried shells after they have dried.

Weighing one capsule. Take the things out. Now weigh the empty shells. This is done by deducting the weight of the shells from the weight of the whole capsule to get the net weight of its contents. An additional 19 capsules are used for the process.

By adding the individual net weights, the average net weight is calculated. Determined for each capsule is the percentage variation from the mean net weight.

Individual net weight variations shouldn't go above the following guidelines.

Average weight of tablets	**Deviation (%)**	**Number of tablets**
Less than 80 mg	±10.0 ±20.0	Minimum 18 Maximum 2
80 mg to 250 mg	±7.5 ±15.0	Minimum 18 Maximum 2
More than 250 mg	±5.0 ±10.0	Minimum 18 Maximum 2

1. **Disintegration Test:** For this, the USP disintegration device is employed. The device is made up of six 3 inch long glass tubes that are open at the top and are pressed up against a 10-mesh screen at the bottom of the basket rack assembly. One capsule is put into each tube, and the basket rack is placed in a medium that is the right temperature—37.2°C—so that the capsules remain 2.5 cm below the liquid's surface on their upward movements and don't get any closer to the bottom of the beaker on their downward movements. At a frequency of 28 to 32 cycles per minute, the basket assembly housing the capsules oscillates up and down over a distance of 5 to 6 cm. Use the device for the allotted amount of time. The capsule passes the test if it disintegrates within the allotted time and all particles pass through the 10-mesh screen.

If every capsule has completely broken apart, the capsule passes the test. Repeat the test on 12 more capsules if 1 or 2 fail to completely dissolve. If at least 16 out of the total of 18 capsules examined disintegrate, the criteria has been met.

CAPSULES	DISINTEGRATION TIME
Hard capsule	30
Soft capsule	60

7. **Dissolution Test**: The USP dissolving apparatus is the same for tablets and capsules. The dissolution test apparatus consists of a 1000 ml capacity cylindrical glass or clear plastic jar with a hemispherical bottom. The vessel has a temperature of 0.5. A lid with four holes is attached to the vessel that is partially submerged in water and whose temperature is maintained at 370 degrees. One hole is for the shaft, one is for the thermometer, and the remaining two are for sample. The shaft is connected to a motor with variable speed that turns between 25 and 150 revolutions per minute.

Fill the vessel with 1000 cc of dissolution media (water devoid of dissolved air). The vessel is submerged in water. A constant 37 °C is maintained. Put the required number of capsules in the dry basket. Start the motor, and set the speed to 100 rpm or the amount specified in the monograph. Sample is withheld and filtered at the predetermined period described in the monograph. To maintain a consistent volume, replenish the volume taken out for sample with new dissolving medium. To determine the amount of drug dissolved, the samples are examined using analytical techniques like UV and chromatography.

If neither S1 nor S2 results are consistent, continue testing through the next two stages. The amount Q. is the specified concentration of the dissolved active ingredient, given as a proportion of the declared content.

Stage	Number units	Acceptance criteria
S1	6	Each unit is not less than Q* + 5%
S2	6	Average of the 12(S1+S2) units is ≥ and no unit less than Q – 15%
S3	12	Average of 24 (S1+S2+S3) units is ≥ Q and not more than 2 units are less than Q-15 % and no units is less than Q-25%

*Q is the amount of dissolved active ingredient specified in the individual monograph, expressed as a percentage of the labeled content.

STABILITY TESTING:

- **Moisture Permeation Test**:To check if single-unit and unit dose containers are suitable for packaging capsules, this test is performed to ascertain their moisture permeability characteristics. A desiccant pellet that reveals the color is packed with the dosing unit. Over the course of the designated time, the packaged item was exposed to known relative humidity. Check for color changes in the desiccant pellet. Any alteration in hue suggests moisture absorption. Calculations can be made to determine the weight of the pellet as compared to the pretest weight.

- **Physical Stability**: Unprotected soft gelatin capsules quickly establish equilibrium with the storage environment's air conditions.
- This innate quality justifies a quick examination of how temperature and humidity affect the products.

• Generalizations about the effects of temperature and humidity on soft gelatin capsules must be limited to a control capsule that contains mineral oil and is made of a gelatin shell with a dry glycerin to dry gelatin ratio of 0.5 to 1 and a dry gelatin to water ratio of 1 to 1, dried to equilibrium at 20 to 30 percent RH and 21 to 24°C.

•The pick-up or loss of water by the capsule shell is principally responsible for the physical stability of soft gelatin capsules.

•The above-controlled capsule should be physically stable enough at temperatures ranging from just above freezing to as high as 600°C, assuming that these are avoided by suitable packaging.

. • The moisture content of capsules is picked up more when the humidity rises. For instance: Gelatin retains around 12 percent (48 mg) of water at 30 percent RH at ambient temperature, while glycerin retains 7 percent (14 mg) of water. At 60 percent RH, the moisture content should be 17.4 percent. More significant impacts on the capsule shell are produced at higher humidity levels (> 60% RH at 21 to 240°C). Accelerated stability tests are regularly carried out by the capsule producer on new products as a crucial component of the manufacturing development procedure.

• The ideal conditions for testing are

(a) 80 percent relative humidity at room temperature in an open container

(b) 400 degrees Celsius in an open container

(c) 400 degrees Celsius in a closed container.

• The capsule should be adjusted to known humidity levels before testing, ideally between 20 and 30 percent RH at 21 and 24 degrees Celsius.

. •Only after the capsules have stabilized at room temperature should the findings of the heat test previously described be evaluated.

Stability: RH of 20–30% at a temperature of 21–24 °C.

Temperature	Humidity	Effect on capsule shell
21-24^{0}C	60%	Capsules becomes softer, tackier, and bloated.
Greater than 24^{0}C	Greater than 45%	More rapid and pronounced effect.

Packaging and Storage of Soft Gelatin Capsules

•Capsules should be stored in a cold, well-ventilated glass or plastic container.

•Compared to cardboard boxes, these sorts of containers are easier to handle, carry, and protect the capsules from moisture and dust.

•A tuft of cotton is placed over and under the capsules in the vials to stop them from rattling.

•To stop the capsules from absorbing too much moisture, desiccant packets containing silica gel or anhydrous calcium chloride may be added to vials containing extremely hygroscopic capsules. Today's capsules are strip wrapped, allowing for easy counting and identification as well as sanitary handling of medications.

• screw-top plastic bottle (most popular package in USA).

•Clam shell blister: a single-piece, self-locking piece of plastic that doesn't need to be heated.

• Blister box (heat sealed blister on a cardboard).

• Plastic bucket or pail (economical bulk package).

• Zip-locked plastic bag (for sale via retail stores or route trucks must be packed in outer case for shipping).

APPLICATIONS

• As a dose form for oral use.

• As a dosing form for suppositories.

•For topical, ophthalmic, and rectal ointments, as a customized package in tube form, for use in humans and animals.

•It is employed with water-immiscible, volatile and non-volatile liquids such ether, esters, alcohol, organic acids, vegetable and aromatic oils, and aromatic and aliphatic hydrocarbons.

• Solids can also be suspended in a liquid solvent, powdered, granulated, or pelletized, or they can be placed in soft gelatin capsules as a dry substance.

MARKETED FORMULATION OF SOFT GELATIN CAPSULE

S.No	Generic Name	Brand Name	Uses
1	Vitaminum-A 2500	Retinol palmitate 2500	Prevention of vitamin A deficiency.
2	Vitamin-E synthetic 400mg	DL – α Tocopherol acetate 400	Drug applied in vitamin E deficiency.
3	Lecithin 300 mg	Lecithin 300 mg	Lipid metabolism disorder.
4	Methoxsalen	Oxsoralen - Ultra	Used in patients with severe, disabling psoriasis.
5	Lukatret 10 mg	Tretinoin	In treatment of Acute Promyelocytic Leukemia.
6	Entericare	Entericare	It provide sustained delivery
7	Quali-V	Quali V	For eventual use in pharmaceutical products.

REFERENCES:-

- *Theory and Practice of Industrial Pharmacy by Liberman & Lachman, 3rd edition , Pg no 398-411*
- *Allen L. and Ansel H. (2014). Ansel's Pharmaceutical Dosage Forms and Drug Delivery Systems. Philadelphia: Lipincott Williams and Wilkins. Page no 249-255*
- *Kawabata, Y.; Wada, K.; Nakatani, M.; Yamada, S.; Onoue, S. Formulation design for poorly water-soluble drugs based on biopharmaceutics classification system: Basic approaches and practical applications. Int. J. Pharm. 2011, 420, 1–10. [CrossRef] [PubMed]*

CHAPTER VI

PELLETS

Pellets: They are compact (0.5-1.5 mm), freely flowing spherical units produced by pelletizing fine powder or pharmaceuticals and excipient granules in bulk.

Pelletization: Fine powders or granules of excipients and bulk medications are combined to form pellets by an agglomeration process.

Cryopelletization: It is a process that turns a liquid droplet into a solid, spherical particle using liquid nitrogen.

INTRODUCTION

These are the small size (0.5-1.5 mm), free-flowing, spherical units produced by pelletizing procedures on fine powder or granules of bulk medicines and excipients. Low porosity describes pellets (about 10 percent).

Pellets may be compacted into disintegrating tablets or packed in firm gelatin capsules. Pellets designed for oral usage swiftly release their contents in the stomach, spread throughout the gastrointestinal tract, and maximize drug absorption while minimizing local irritation.

Pellets

ADVANTAGES

- **Uniformity of dose**- Extrusion-speronization and layering procedures provide excellent accuracy for medication administration in pellets.
- Spheres offer **superior flow characteristics**. In automated processes or those requiring precise dosing, such as tableting, moulding operations, capsule filling, and packing, this becomes quite helpful.
- **Preventing the production of dust** improving process safety because fine powders might produce dust explosions and health issues when breathed in.
- Pellets may be applied with **controlled release because of their perfect low surface area** to volume ratio, which creates the optimal form for applying film coatings.

• They can be used in combination to provide incompatible bioactive chemicals simultaneously, provide distinct release patterns at the **same or separate locations in the gastrointestinal (GI) tract**, or do all three at once.

THERAPEUTIC ADVANTAGES

- Following administration, pellets can **move around freely inside the GIT, resulting in maximum medication absorption.**

• The widespread distribution of **spherical particles in the GI tract inhibits localized drug build-up** and reduces some drugs‘ unpleasant effects on the gastric mucosa.

- **Decrease both intra- and inter-patient variability.**
- Modified-release Compared to single-unit dosage forms, **multiparticulate delivery systems are less prone to dose dumping.**

DISADVANTAGE

- The process of filling pellets involves filling capsules, which might raise prices.
- Pellets' film coating is destroyed during tableting.
- The pellets‘ sizes might vary from formulation to formulation, however they typically range between 0.05 mm and 2 mm.
- Pellets are too stiff to easily be compressed into tablets. As a result, they are frequently given to patients in hard gelatin capsules.
- Pelletization necessitates highly specialized equipment, which raises the cost of production.
- Having too many process and formulation variables makes it difficult to control the production process.

DESIRABLE PROPERTIES OF PELLETS

- For Uncoated pellets:

a. uniform size of the sphere
b. A small particle size range
c. Good flow characteristics
d. Minimal friability,
e. An even surface
f. Less production of dust
g. Reproducible packing
h. Good flow properties
I. Easily coated

For Coated pellets:
a. Maintain all above properties
b. Desirable drug release characteristics

FORMULATION REQUIREMENTS

Excipients used in pellet dosage forms are frequently the same as those used in tablet and capsule dosage forms.

1. **Fillers**: They are utilized to give products more bulk and make it simpler for consumers to take very little active ingredients. They often consist of insoluble or water-soluble materials. The target dose, a drug's physical characteristics, and the production method all influence the filler choice. MCC (Micro Crystalline Cellulose), starch, sucrose, lactose, and mannitol, as an example.

2. **Binders**: They are included to bind powder and create the integrity of pellets. Examples include sucrose, starch, hydroxypropyl methyl cellulose, gelatin, pyrrolidone, methyl cellulose, and polyvinyl.

3. **Lubricants**: They are included to lessen friction between the equipment's surface and the particles. For instance, glycerin, polyethylene glycol, calcium and magnesium stearate

4. **Separating agents**: Pellets may accumulate surface charges during manufacture and become attracted to one another. Pellets are encouraged to separate into discrete units using separating agents. Example: Kaolin, Talc, and Silicon Dioxide

5. **Disintegrating agents**. Ex. Alginate, cross carmellose sodium.

6. **pH adjuster**: Ex. Citrate, Phosphate, Meglumine

7. **Surfactant**: To increase wettability by reducing the interfacial tension between the liquid and drug particles, surfactants are added to the liquid. Surfactants aid in weakening the liquid bridges, making pellets more friable. Ex. Polysorbate, Sodium Lauryl Sulfate

8. **Spheronization enhancer**. In addition to giving the formulation flexibility, they also give it binding qualities, which are crucial for pellet strength and integrity. Example: Sodium carboxymethylcellulose; microcrystalline cellulose.

9. **Glidant:** They either reduce friction during the compression process or during the ejection phase between the die wall and the material mix. Moreover, they significantly contribute to the pellets' smooth discharge from the Spheronizer Ex. Talc, starch, and magnesium stearate

10. **Release modifier**: They are simultaneously introduced to possess certain release profiles. In order to improve drug release kinetics, formulations typically include water-soluble low molecular weight excipients, surfactants, and disintegrants. In contrast, pellets frequently contain hydrophobic materials, inorganic salts, and water-insoluble polymers that swell or gel. Example: Carnauba wax, Shellac, and ethyl cellulose.

11. **Others**: Agents for flavoring, coloring, and sweetness are included.

PELLETIZATION PROCESS

Pelletization is an agglomeration process that turns tiny powders or granules of bulk medications and excipients into microscopic, free-flowing, semi-spherical particles. Spherical agglomerate preparation can be validated using a variety of techniques

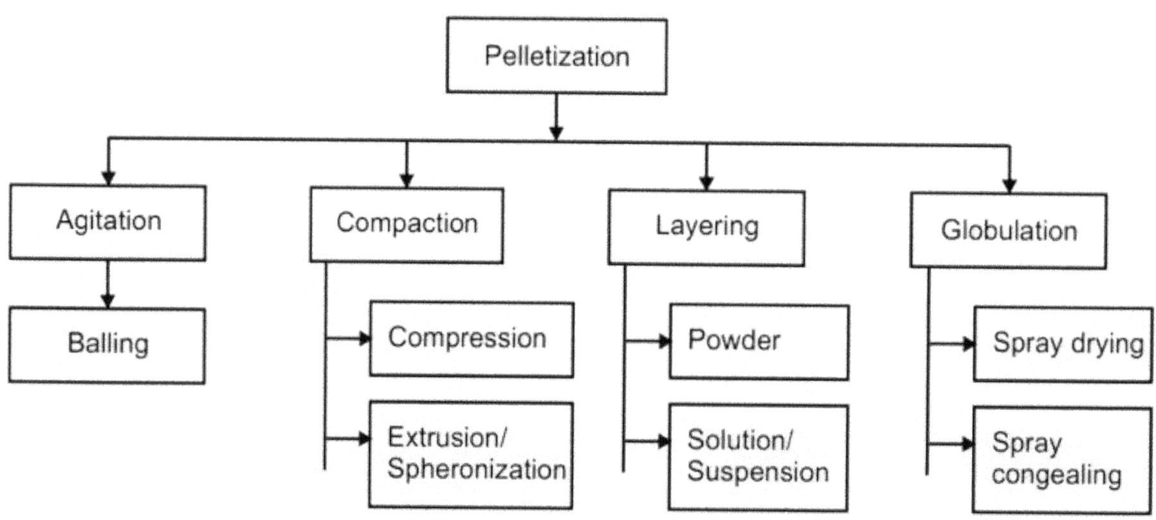

Figure: Pelletization Process

1. **Agitation (Balling)**

Another name for this is spherical aggregation. The necessary liquid is introduced to the finely separated particles before or during the agitation in this pelletization procedure. This mass produces spherical particles when it is continuously rolled or tumbled in pans, discs, drums, or mixers.

In the liquid-induced agglomeration method, liquid is introduced to powder to produce agglomerates, whereas the binding substance is in melt form in the melt-induced agglomeration method. The iron ore and fertilizer industries are the principal users of this technique.

2. **Compaction:**

A) Compression: It is a pelletization process in which mixtures or blends of active ingredients and excipients are compacted

B) Extrusion Spheronization: It was first made available in the early 1960s. This technique frequently used in the pharmaceutical business to create spheroids with a diameter of about 1 mm. It is particularly beneficial for producing dense, spherical pellets with high drug loading that are homogeneous in size and shape for controlled-release oral solid dosage forms.

3. **Layering:** This procedure involves coating starting or nonpareil seeds with medication in powder, solution, or suspension form. A different-composition outer shell and an interior core region make up the finished pellet. There are two categories for this process.

A. Powder layering

B. Solution or Suspension layering

A. Powder Layering:

This approach involves coating prepared cores or nuclei with successive layers of powdered drug, excipient, or both, with the aid of a binding agent. To ensure equilibrium, the binding solution and the finely ground powder are added simultaneously and carefully.

In the earliest steps, a liquid bridge made from a spray binding liquid connects the medication particle to the beginning seeds to create the pellets. During the process of solidification, these liquid bridges are swapped out with solid ones. With this procedure, the medication and binder solution are formed in layers until the required pellet size is reached.

The standard coating pan was the first piece of machinery used to produce pellets on a large scale, but it has some serious drawbacks, including a highly ineffective drying process and very little mixing. Thus, tangential spray granulators and centrifugal bed granulators are both employed nowadays.

B. Solution/Suspension Layering:

In this method, beginning seeds—which could be inert materials or granule crystals of the same medication—are covered with successive layers of solution and/or suspension of pharmacological compounds and binders.

This method involves dissolving or suspending medication particles and other components in the binding liquid. When the fluid or suspension is sprayed onto the muscles, the droplets impinge on the beginning seeds or cores and disseminate uniformly. Solid bridges are created between successive layers of drug substances or polymers as well as between the nucleus and the first layer of drug substances during drying. This procedure should be repeated until the required drug or polymer layer is created. As a result, making pellets using a normal coating press, a centrifugal fluidized bed granulator, or a Wurster coating has proved successful. This process uses a cutting-edge fluidized bed technology to layer or dissolve neutral pellets. The three-component spray nozzle from Hüettlin is a wise choice since it prevents the nozzle from clogging or drying out the spray too much. Droplet formation or globulation: Spray drying, and spray congealing are included in globulation, or droplet creation, in this technique. The atomization of hot melt, solutions, or suspension results in the creation of spherical pellets.

EQUIPMENTS USED

- **Extrusion spheronization:**

- In the creation of sustained-release, controlled-release delivery systems, extrusion spheronization is often used.
- The primary goal of extrusion spheronization is to create uniformly sized pellets or spheroids with a high medication loading capacity.

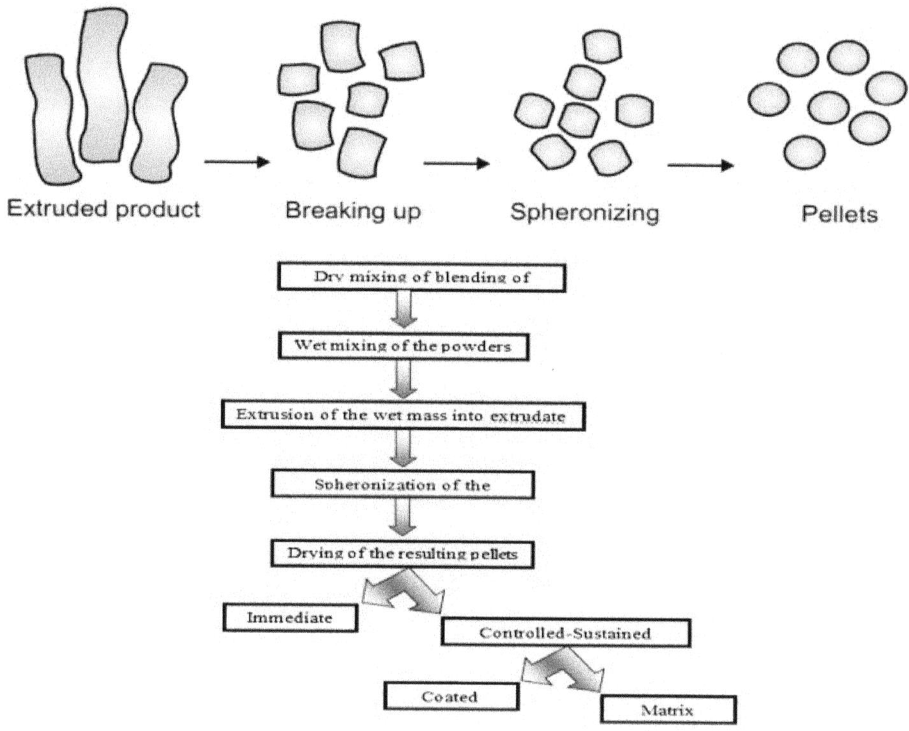

Figure: Extrusion/Spheronization

a. Dry mixing: To achieve homogenous powder dispersion, a variety of mixer types including twin shell blenders, high shear mixers, tumbler mixers, and planetary mixers are employed.

b. Wet Massing: This creates a plastic mass suitable for extrusion. With the granulation end point being the only difference, it is comparable to the traditional wet granulation process. The behavior of the wet mass extrusion operation determines the granulation end point. The Horbat mixer, the Planetory mixer, the Sigma blade mixer, and the high shear mixer are the most often used granulators. For routine mixing and granulation tasks, a planetary mixer is employed.

c.Extrusion: In this method, rod-shaped particles of uniform diameter are created by feeding a moist mass through an extruder. When the extrudate is rolled during the spheronization process, it should be enough plastic to deform but not too much so that the extrudate particles stick to other particles.

d. Spheronization: It is a procedure that makes use of the spheronizer. The extrudate is rotated at a higher speed by friction plates in the spheronizer to transform these rod-shaped particles into spherical particles with a constrained size distribution.

e. Drying: It is the stage where the pellets are dried to maintain their shape and size in a tray drier, a fluidized bed dryer, or at a higher temperature.

f. Screening: In order to obtain the desired size distribution, it is done. For this, sieves are employed.

- **HOT MELT EXTRUSION:**

Hot melt extrusion is a method that uses controlled pressure to push raw materials through a die to create products with a homogeneous shape and density.

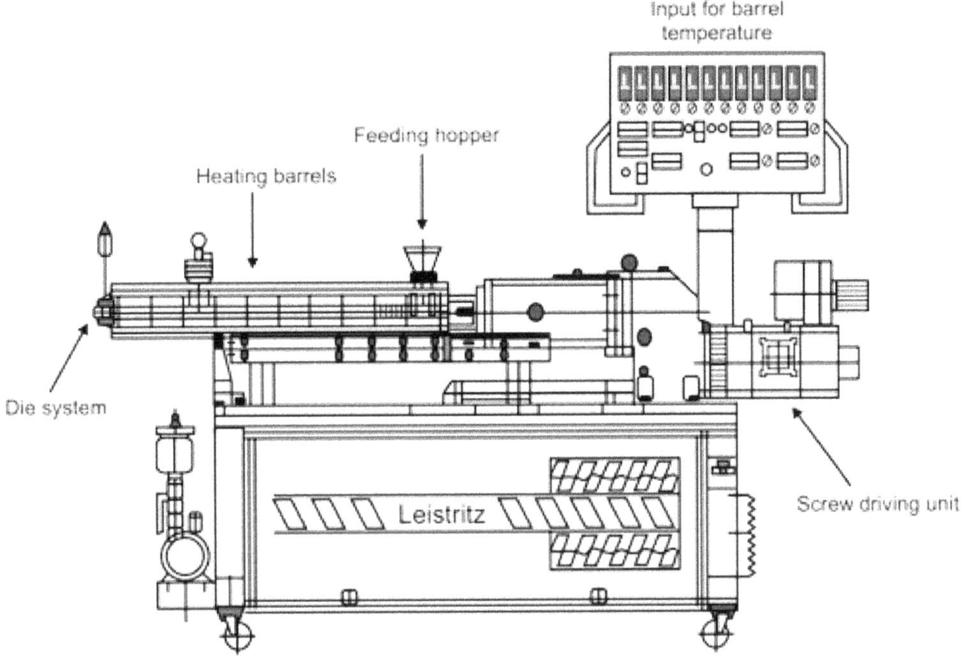

Figure:Hot-melt Extrusion

As a result, the four phases of the flow process are often used to provide a theoretical foundation for comprehending the melt extrusion process:

1.The extruder's feeding.

2. Transporting of mass (mixing and reduction of particle size).

3 Flowing through the dye

4. Exit the die and move on to downstream processing.

Applications of Extrusion in the Pharmaceutical Industry:

There are a number of uses for melt extrusion in the pharmaceutical sector, including

1. By creating a solid dispersion or solid solution, the drug's rate of dissolution and bioavailability are increased.
2. Modifying or controlling the drug's release.
3. Covering off an active drug's unpleasant taste.

- **Granulation :**

Wet Granulation:

• Powders are mixed with dry primary powder particles using a granulating fluid before being added to a liquid solution. A solvent that must be volatile is present in the fluid.

• satisfies the physical requirements for tablet compression.

Fluid-bed Granulation:

• A fluid-bed granulator constantly runs the process.

• The suspended particles are sprayed with a granulation solution, which causes them to quickly dry in the hot air stream.

1. **Fluid-Bed Granulation**:

The steps for performing fluid-bed granulation are as follows: (Tangential-Spray Method)

- Pre-blending the formulation powder in an airflow, along with the active compounds, fillers, and disintegrants.
- A suitable liquid binder is sprayed onto the fluidized (suspended) powder bed to create the mixture's granules.
- granular product is dried to the proper moisture content.

Parameters:

- Equipment parameters
- Product parameters
- Process parameters

Advantages over Traditional Wet Granulation:

- Automated completed in a single unit, reducing money, time, and transfer losses.
- The fluid bed granulation procedure increases the effectiveness of tablet dissolution for both nimodipine and spiro

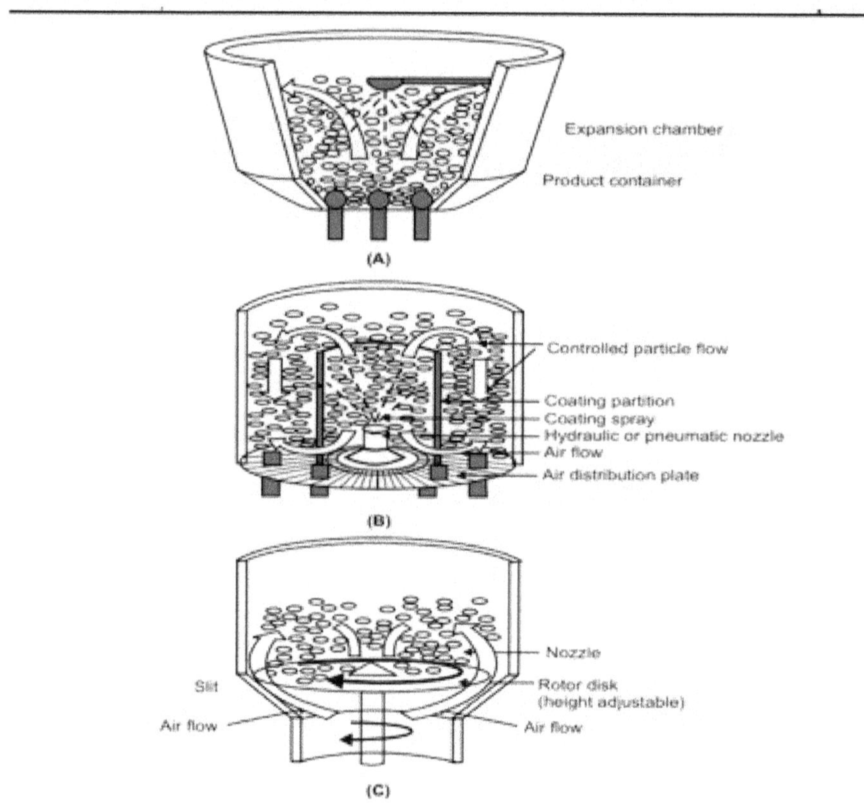

Figure: Three versions of fluidized bed granulator

1. **Melt Granulation:**

Addition of a meltable binder produces granulation. At room temperature, the binder is solid, but between 50 and 80 °C, it melts. Polyethylene Glycol (PEG) 2000, 4000, 6000, and 8000, for instance (40 - 60o C).

- The melted binder then functions as a liquid binder.
- Since dried granules can be made by simply cooling an object to room temperature, there is no requirement for a drying process.

SPRAY DRYING:

Drug entities (in solution or suspension) with or without excipients are sprayed into a heated air stream to create dry, extremely spherical particles in this procedure. It is typically used to increase the bioavailability of poorly soluble medicines by increasing their dissolving rates.

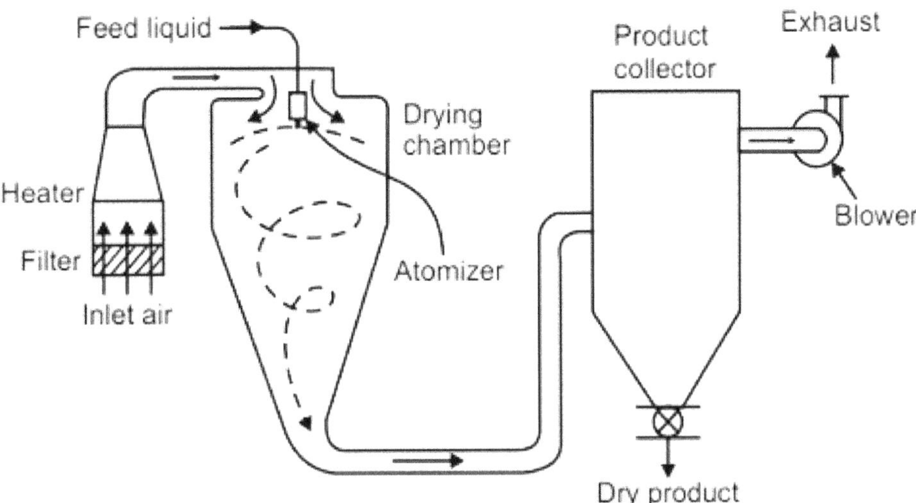

Figure: Spray Dryer

SPRAY CONGEALING OR SPRAY CHILLING :

This procedure involves allowing a medication to melt, disperse, or dissolve in hot melts of gums, waxes, fatty acids, etc. It is then sprayed into an air chamber with a temperature that is below the melting points of the constituent parts of the formulation. Similar to spray drying, this method does not require a heat source. Under the right processing conditions, this procedure is utilized to produce sphere-shaped congealed pellets. To obtain a sustained releasing effect, this procedure is performed.

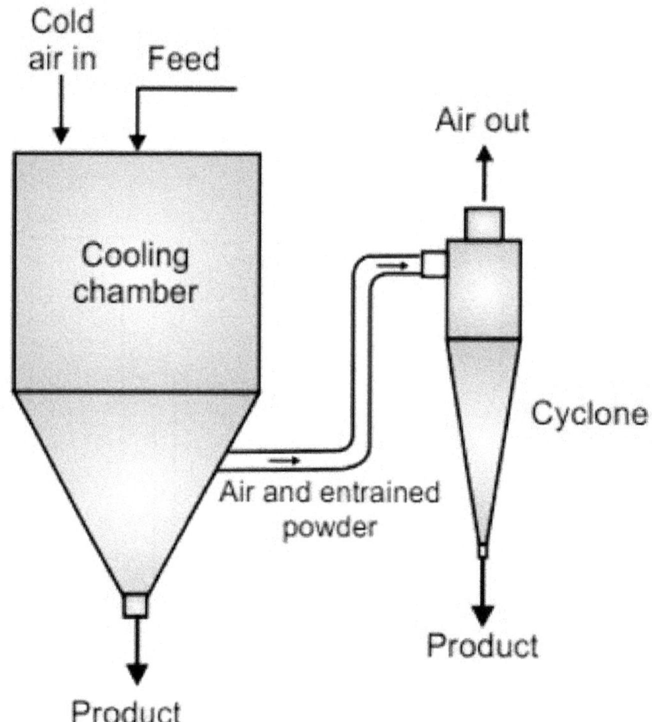

Figure: Spray-congealing

<u>EXAMPLE OF DRUG MARKETED AS PALLETS</u>

S.No	Drugs	Manufacturer	Product	Therapeutic class
1	Omeprazole magnesium	Astra Zeneca	Losec MUPS	Antiulcer
2	Esomeprazole magnesium	Astra Zeneca	Esomeprazole	Antiulcer
3	Metoprolol tartrate	Astra Zeneca	Toprol XL	Antihypertensive
4	Lansoprazole	Takeda	Prevacid solu Tab	Antiulcer
5	Theophylline	Key	Theodur	Antiasthmatic

<u>REFERENCES</u>

- *Ghebre-Sellassiel, Knoch A. Pelletization Techniques. In Swarbric kJ, Editor. Encyclopedia of Pharmaceutical Technology, 3° Edition: Informa Healthcare; 2000. P. 2651-63.*
- *Hirjau M, Nicoara AC, Hirjau V, Lupuleasa D. Pelletization techniques used in pharmaceutical fields. Practica Farmaceutică 2011; 4 (3-4): 206-11.*
- *Ghai D. Pelletization: An Alternate to Granulation Pharma Times 2011January; 43 (1) 2011: 13-15.*

CHAPTER VII

PARENTERAL PRODUCT

Definition

Parenteral products are administered directly into the blood circulation in human body, these include administration through skin or mucus membrane and does not include administration methods that are through mouth or oral.

- They are pyrogen-free and sterile preparations.
- These are prepared in various liquid (suspensions, emulsions, or solutions) or solid dosage forms.
- The term parenteral is derived from Greek word Para- outside and Enterone- intestine.
- J. D. Major and Johannes Elsholtz were first who successfully injected humans in 1662 using solution of opium.

<u>Types of Parenterals-</u>

Based on route of administration, the types of parenterals are:

1. Intravenous (IV) – injected through vein
2. Intramuscular (IM) – It is generally performed by joint injection.
3. Subcutaneous (SC) – under the skin
4. Intradermal (ID)- Into the skin
5. Intraarticular – into the joints
6. Intracerebral- into the cerebrum
7. Intraarterial- performed on arteries
8. Intra cardia- into the heart
9. Intracarvernous- at the base of penis
10. Endotracheal- down the trachea
11. Intra vaginal -in the vagina
12. Intra spinal – into the spinal column

There are other types of parenteral like perivascular administration, transmucosal, transdermal, intravitreal, intravesical, intrauterine, intraocular, etc.

Based on dosage forms-

1. solutions
2. suspensions
3. emulsions
4. dry prowders

<u>Advantages Of Parenteral-</u>

1. Rapid onset of action.
2. Prolonged drug action.
3. Helpful in case of unconscious patients.
4. Drugs which are undergoing extensive first pass metabolism are given parenterals which avoid first pass metabolism.
5. These drugs are stable in GIT.

6. Better drug bioavailability.
7. Patient friendly, i.e. patient compliance problem can be avoided.

Disadvantages of Parenterals-

1. Painful injectables.
2. Medical expert is required for administration.
3. Improper dosing is common in case of parenteral drugs.
4. They show more number of adverse effects.
5. These drugs are irreversible.
6. Manufacturing and packaging of these drugs are more costly.
7. Blood clotting can be seen.

Pre-formulation factors and other essential requirements-

Pre-formulation – These studies are performed in order to find the criteria required for formulating a most stable molecule. Pre-formulation factors are:

1. Solubility-

Solubility of the drug is a major challenge to be studied that must be conducted. There are many ways to enhance the solubility of a drug which is poorly soluble. Some of them are listed below:

a. Molecules can be uncharged or charged in a solution and salt forms are more soluble than uncharged species, thereby creating an ionic salt form, the solubility of the drug can be increased or enhanced.

a. The pH of the solution has an impact on the solubility of poorly soluble drug. And if pH changes, different species in the solution can either get protonated or deprotonated. This may change the charge on the molecule and thus changing the solubility in water.

c. Co-solvents also have an impact on the solubility of less soluble drug. As we know "like dissolves like", therefore drugs which are poorly soluble in water can have better solubility in those solvents. For that solvent screening studies have done, various concentrations of different solvents are prepared, and insoluble drug is added to the point of saturation. The samples are removed, and the undissolved drug is filtered out of the solution, the drug concentration is measured using techniques like HPLC or UV/Vis. Thus, a graph can be generated.
d. Stability –

Thermal stability of bulk drug cab be determined by placing drug samples into dark, nitrogen purged environment and exposing it to various temperatures for some time. Samples are taken out at regular time intervals and using stability indicating method i.e HPLC, degradation of sample is tested.

3. pKa/pH

Solubility is general function of pKa of salt and its chemical nature. So we can state that if pKa od a medium is less than pH of that medium, dissolution can be achieved. Therefore, by determining these factors one can make a parenteral dosage form.

Also, a precaution must be taken while designing a dosage form, although co-solvents can increase the solubility but they may shift the pKa of the buffer by conjugating with the acid base system. Thus affecting the integrity of the dosage form.

4. Solid state characteristics-

Drug can exists in crystalline or amorphous forms, but a combination form of a drug may provide a dosage form with benefits like rapid onset and prolong duration of action. Eg- lente insulin.

Other essential requirements that need to be analyzed before formulation are:

1. Optical activity
2. Melting point
3. pH stability profile
4. thermal stability
5. ionization constant
6. solubility profile
7. potential for polymorphism

Vehicles and Additives-

Vehicles

Vehicles used can be aqueous(water for injection) or non-aqueous(eg- ethyl alcohol, almond oil). Ideal properties of vehicles used are:

1. Must be pharmacological inert and non toxic.
2. Compatible with blood
3. Physically and chemically stable.
4. Must not affect the pH.
5. Should be free from pyrogen.
6. Particulate contamination and colour change must be visually inspected.
7. Must maintain the solubility of API.

Additives

These are added top enhance the product atability. These include antioxidants, chelating agents, solubilizers, buffers etc.

1. Must be non toxic
2. Must not adversely affect the product.
3. Should not interfere with the therapeutic efficacy of the drug.
4. Must be evaluated before formulation.

Importance of isotonicity-

Compounds which are isotonic in nature help in reducing the pain of injection in an area. Such agents are sodium chloride, and other sodium salts and non-electrolytes such as glycerin and lactose.

Parenteral products must isotonic otherwise it may lead to haemolysis or RBC.

If the solution injected is hypertonic then it cause shrinkage of RBCs and if the solution injected is hypotonic then it may lead to swelling of RBCs.

Tonicity adjusters are added if solution is still not isotonic i.e. <280 mOsm/ kg as measured by osmometer.

Production procedure, production facilities and aseptic procedure-

Production procedure-

1. Cleaning of equipment and containers at parenteral product manufacturing area
2. Collection of raw material or dispensing

3. Preparation of bulk solution.
4. Then QC analysis will take place, if passed then send for pre-filtration.
5. Sterile filtration will be carried.
6. Filling
7. Half stoppering
8. Lyophilization i.e., freeze drying
9. Full stoppering
10. Sealing
11. Again, QC will perform analysis, if passed the undergo inspection
12. Packaging and shipment

Zones as per gazette of india:
Black zone- storage
Grey zone- weighing, dissolution and filtration.
White zone- filling of parenterals.
Zones as per the C GMP:
Zone 1- exterior
Zone2- warehouse
Zone3- general production.
Zone4- clean area
Zone5- weighing, mixing and transfer area.
Zone6- filling area
Zone7- filling line.
Production facilities and controls-

1. Primary objective must be the prevention from contamination.
2. Ceramic- plastic is best material for floors.
3. Spray -on-tile is ceramic material used for forming continuous, smooth, seal coating on the walls and ceilings.
4. HEPA filtered laminar flow is fitted in clean room for better environmental conditions.
5. Hard surfaced, non-porous, preferably stainless-steel furniture is used.
6. For better lightening and supervisory view of operations, glass is used in partition.
7. The material used for ceiling, walls and floors should be non-porous and easy to clean.
8. Air showers are provided before entering the controlled area in order to reduce the chances of contamination from outside.
9. There are garment cubicles or cabinets which are provided with U.V. germicidal tube to ensure keeping the garments free from bacteria etc.
10. PVC Flaps or swing doors are fitted in a parenteral production area.

<u>Aseptic processing-</u>
For aseptic processing there are types of operations to be carried out in various grades:
GRADE A- aseptic preparation and filling.
GRADE B- background room conditions for activities requiring grade A.
GRADE C- solution is prepared for filtration.
GRADE D- compound handling after washing.
Role of environmental monitoring in aseptic processing-
There are cGMP and FDA guidelines on types of monitoring for aseptic dispensing facilities.

1. Sessional test- For record duration of session.

2. Daily test- For recording pressure drop across HEPA filter and recording pressure differential between aseptic room and adjacent area.
3. Weekly test
4. Monthly test- In this air borne viable organism in LAFC or isolator is checked.
5. Annual test- For integrity and efficiency of all HEPA filters.

Formulation of injections, sterile powders, large volume parenteral and lyophilised product-

6. Formulations of injections-

Injections are sterile solutions of drugs in oily vehicle that are injected into the body. These must be pyrogen free, sterile and isotonic. There are various routes of administrating injectables as studies in section 4.1.1
In the preparation of injections, various substances are added to prepare are stable parenteral preparation-

- Vehicles
- Solubilizing agents
- Buffer agents
- Stabilizers
- Chelating agents. Etc.

Example – Formulation of diazepam for 5mg/ml injection.

Ingredients	Quantity
Diazepam	500mg
Propylene glycol	40ml
Ethyl alcohol	10ml
Sodium benzoate	4.9mg
Benzoic acid	100mg
Benzyl alcohol	1.5ml
Sterile water	q.s. 100ml

2. **Formulation of sterile powders.**

Three methods for such formulation are-

- Sterile recrystallization- In this a drug is dissolved in solvent and the solution is sterilized by 0.22 micrometre membrane filter. Then to crystallize the drug, a sterile anti- solvent is added and filtered and dried.
- Spray drying- In the drug solution is sprayed in dry chamber where it comes in contact with a hot steam of sterile gas (80-100 degree Celsius)
- Lyophilization- In this drug solution is filtered into trays that are loaded aseptically into a freeze dryer. After that solution is frozen at -50°C and with the help of vacuum it is dried and separated.

3. **Formulation of large volume parenteral-**

LVP are pyrogen free and sterile injected products that are packed in large volume i.e. more than 100ml.
Dosage unit- single
Preservative- not used
Buffers- not used
Formulation- solution and o/w nutrient emulsion
Isotonicity- should be present
Uses- nutrition, detoxification and in surgery.
LVP contains following-

- Hyperalimentation solution- nutritional-proteins- lipid emulsions.
- Cardioplegia solution
- Peritoneal dialysis- for removing toxic substances from body.
- Irrigating solution- used for irrigation, flushing and aid in cleansing body cavities.

LVP formulation contains-

- API- drug
- Vehicle- aqueous or non-aqueous, solid vehicle
- Adjuvants- tonicity adjusters:

Electrolyte, Nacl (0.5%-0.9%)
Non-electrolyte, dextrose (4-5%)

- Buffers – acetate/citrate (pH 3-6)

Phosphate (pH 6-8)
Glutamate (pH 8-10)

- Anti-oxidants- 0.1-0.5%
- Preservatives- 1-2%
- Complexing agents- 0.01-0.05%
- Antimicrobial agents- 0.01%

Example of LVP- Drip is a second type of LVP solution which is used for continuous delivery of IV medication to treat specific condition.

Containers and closure selection, filling and sealing of ampoules, vials and infusion fluids-

Containers-

They are in close contact with the drug, hence container used for packaging of a particular drug must not affect the stability of the product. Moreover, physical characteristics of a container is most likely to be considered first before the selection of a packaging material of a drug. Types of containers used are :

7. Plastic containers-

For the preparations of ophthalmic solutions, LVP and SVP parenteral plastic contaoiners are used. And the main ingredient or material used for production of such plastic containers is thermoplastic polymer.

Widely used plastic container is of **polypropylene** as it can only withstand sterilization by autoclaving. It is translucent, has high surface gloss and abrasion resistant.

Flexible **polyethylene** containers are used for ophthalmic solutions to be administrated in drops and **polyvinylchloride** bags for IV solutions.

Advantages-

- Non breakable
- Less weight as compared to glass
- Less transportation cost
- Flexible.

Disadvantages-

- Adversely affected by elevated temperature.
- Reactivity due to absorption and adsorption can occur.
- Not as clear as glass

8. Glass containers-

These are mostly composed of silicon dioxide tetrahedron, and are modified physiochemically by oxides of sodium, potassium, calcium, magnesium etc. Almost all injectavles are packed in glass containers.

Glass containers are classified on the bases of hydrolytic resistance-

- Type I / borosilicate- known as neutral glass. It is chemically inert and have high hydrolytic resistance. It is used for all parenteral preparations. It consists of: 81% silicon dioxide, 13% boric oxide and other oxides.
- Type II / sodalime treated glass- have high hydrolytic resistance and is composed of silicon dioxide and sodium oxide14% , calcium oxide 18%.
- Type III / sodalime glass
- Type IV / NP glass – used for oral dosages.

Closure selection –

These are the stoppers or bungs that form a part of the container closure system. **Rubber-** they maintainthe sterility and helps in prevention from contamination when needle is inserted in it. The elastomer used is natural rubber or synthetic rubber such as chlorobutyl rubber or butyl rubber.

Filling parenteral

Filling of liquids- small volume of liquid is filled with the help of stroke of the syringe or plunger. The tube must be able to enter freely into the container and fill it with the liquid drug in such a way that air can be escaped without sweeping the entering liquid.

Filling of emulsions and suspensions- they require special equipments for filling because of their viscosity. Bottle with wide mouth and high pressure is required for obtaining uniform flow rate. For decreasing the viscosity, jacketed reservoir tanks are used as they increase the temperature.

Filling of solids- small granular particles flow is faster than flow of solid materials. Thus machine methods of filling must be employed in case when solid is obtained in relatively free flowing form. This methods involves measurement of volume of solid which is calibrated in terms of weight. Containers having wide mouth are used for filling of solids because of slow flow rate

Vacuum filling- In this method, vacuum in the reservoir draws the liquid through delivery tube into the bottle. And when thre liquid reaches the level of an adjustable overflow tube, seal is mechanically loosened and the vacuum is released.

Sealing ampoules and vials

- Sealing of ampoules- Bead seals or pull seals can be formed by melting a portion of the glass of the neck inorder to close the ampoules. By heating the neck of rotating ampoule below the tip and then pulling the tip away to form twisted small capillary just before melted closed, pull seals can be formed.
- Sealing of vials or bottles- rubber closures must fit the opening of the container snugly enough to produce a seal. Aluminuim caps are used to hold rubber closures in place. And sinhgle caps contain hole /center that torn away at the time of use to expose the rubber closure.
- Sealing of infusion bottles- these are sealed and filled by blow fill and seal technology (BFS). In this the container is formed, filled and sealed in one continuous automated process. Following steps for the same are – parison extrusion

Container moulding
Container sealing
Container discharge.

Quality control tests for parenteral products-

1. **Pyrogen test** – This is done by the LAL test and the Gel Clot method for detection of bacterial endotoxins.

LAL test – The limulus amebocyte test is a test in which an animal limulus polyphemus is used for in-vitro detection of endotoxin in different environment. As this animal experiences coagulation in its haemolymph due to the presence of bacterial endotoxins. This test is only valid for detecting endotoxins and not any other type if microorganism.

2. **Leakage test**- This is used to ensure proper packing of the container so that contents may not be leaked.
3. **Sterility test**- This of used for the detection of microbes present in the produced drug. Following are the methods for performing sterility testing-

Method (A): Membrane filtration method

- Membrane used in this is of pore size 0.45 micrometre and diameter 47 millimetre.
- For strongly alcoholic solutions, cellulose acetate filtrate is used and for weakly alcoholic solutions, cellulose nitrate filtrate is used.
- Using rinsing fluid, membrane is rinsed.
- Then fluid products in pressurized aerosol form are freezed in an alcohol dry ice mixture at least -20 degree Celsius and added prior to transfer of the contents.
- Then after filtration, membrane is cut inyto two equal halves and each half is transferred to culture medium.
- Incubation – fluid thioglycolate medium is incubated at 32 degree Celsius and casein digest medium is incubated at 25 degree Celsius for atleast 14 days
- Medium is examined for microbial growth at intervals. If no growth is found then the product complies with the sterility testing.

And if growth is found then the product does not complies with the sterility testing.

Method (B) Direct inoculation:

- Prepared drug is added to the cultural medium and volume must not bemore than 10%.
- Neutralize the solution by dilution.
- Inoculation
- Incubation not less than 14 days.
- Observe the culture at regular intervals.
- After 14 days, transfer to fresh vessel of the same medium amnd the incubate the original and then transfer vessel for not less than 4 days.

- Results are same as in method (A).

References

1. Lechman Liebermans, fourth edition, The Theory and Practice of Industrial Pharmacy, CBS publishers and distributors.

2. Dr. B. Prakash Rao, Dr. S. Rajarajan, Dr. Beny Baby, (2020) industrial pharmacy I, Nirali Prakashan.

3. Northeast biomanufacturing centre and collaborative, (2012) Introduction to Biomanufacturing chapter 13-Formulation and development of parenteral products.

4. The 10th US-Japan symposium on drug delivery system.FDA centre for Drug Evaluation and Research Data standards Manual: Route of Administration.

CHAPTER VIII

OPHTHALMIC PREPARATIONS

INTRODUCTION

Eye is one of the complicated organs of the human body. Its distinct anatomical structure has always been a topic of interest to the scientists and especially the preparations and formulations made for curing any diseases or for performing any operations related to the eyes. One of the major concerns faced is to improve the bioavailability of such preparations.

This can be improved by increasing the contact time between the preparation and the cornea of the eye. In earlier days the contact time was improved by adding polymers to these eye formulations. Excipients like cyclodextrins which increase drug penetration into the eyeball are now used. Another important aspect here is sustained release of the dosage form which results in the decrease of the frequency of its application.

Ophthalmic preparations are applied on the conjunctiva, conjunctival bags and eyelids. These preparations are generally available in various dosage forms like – suspensions, solutions, colloids (like gel) and ointments.

In this chapter we will learn all about such formulations, method of preparations, evaluation etc.

FORMULATION CONSIDERATIONS

Important aspects that should be kept in mind while preparing an ophthalmic preparation depends on the use of same, for example – ophthalmics used in home, by a professional while performing a surgery in a hospital etc.

Factors which should be considered are-

- Sterility
- Clarity
- Osmolarity
- Stability
- Ph and buffers
- Preservation
- Viscosity
- Type of vehicle used
- Storage and packaging

1. Sterility: There should be no microbial contamination in the ophthalmic formulation. Even a small mistake in the whole process of making the formulation can lead to severe effects on the patient's health including blindness, redness of the eye etc. One of the microbes causing this is *Pseudomonas aeruginosa*. Therefore, it is very important to make the formulation in an aseptic environment and use of laminar air flow cabinet is a must. Here we find similarity in making the parentral and ophthalmic formulations.

1. Clarity: Many constituents are present in ophthalmic preparations, and these should be free from any fine or undissolved particles. Filtration is considered as an important technique which is performed while making such formulations. Properly washed and cleaned equipments should be used in filtration so that the step itself do not add any foreign material in the preparation. In pharmaceutical industries often a test is performed to check for any fine particles or polymers which might be present in the formulation and in this test a visual inspection board is used.

Parameter	Diameter	
Particle size	>/=10 micrometre	> or =25 micrometre
Number of particle	50 per ml	5 per ml

Light Obscuration test Particle Count

3. Osmolarity: It is the solution's concentration or total number of solute particles per litre. Osmolarity plays a major role in determining the stability of the formulations as it acts as a guide of breakdown of a substance in a solution. Human blood plasma has osmolarity in the range of 285-295 milliosmole per kilogram and any variation in the osmolarity of the formulation will have an effect on the eyes.

4. Stability: The stability of any ophthalmic preparation depends on the type of formulation i.e solution or suspension and other factors like pH, preservatives, additives, packaging and storage etc and sometimes one or the other of these factors have to be compromised so as to maintain good stability. For example – pilocarpine and physostigmine works best at a pH of 6.8 but then their expiration date will get decreased to one year at this pH so they are formulated at a pH of 5 which increases the stability by increasing the expiration date to several years. Additives like antioxidants can also be added to enhance the stability by reducing the oxygen sensitivity.

5. Ph and buffers: The ideal pH of any ophthalmic preparation should be 7.4 which is the is pH of the tear fluid of eye but attaining this pH is rarely possible. This is because the API's used in making such preparations are stable at acidic PH. The whole idea is not to provide any discomfort and irritation to the eyes and this can be achieved if the preparation is slightly acidic and if after the application of the formulation the pH of the eye again comes back to 7.4. Buffer capacity is also very important for maintaining the stability and it should be less so as to reduce the amount of irritation.

6. Preservation: Preservatives are inactive ingredients added to the preparations so as to avoid the growth of any microorganisms including bacteria, fungi etc. They should not be causing any discomfort or irritation in the eyes, should work at lower concentrations, should kill a wide variety of microbes and should be stable over different temperature conditions. Types of preservatives – a) Detergents which disrupts the cell membrane and therefore kill the microorganisms. b) Oxidative preservatives which causes oxidative reactions to destroy the cell membrane of the microbes.

Compound class	Example
Quaternary ammoniums	Benzalkonium chloride, Polyquaternium-1
Mercurial	Thiomersal, Phenyl mercuric nitrate, phenyl mercuric acetate
Alcohol	Chlorbutanol, benzyl alcohol
Carboxylic acid	Sorbic acid
Phenols	Methyl/propyl paraben
Amidines	Chlorhexidine
Other	Disodium EDTA

Common Preservatives used for ophthalmic solutions

7. Viscosity: It plays a major role in improving the bioavailability and the contact time of the preparation with the cornea so that the dosage frequency can be reduced and the formulation becomes comfortable for the patients. The corneal contact time can be increased by the thickening of the tear film with the help of polymers which increases the viscosity. Increase in viscosity also slows down the rate of sedimentation the particles and especially in the suspensions in which cake formation can be seen. Example of viscosity enhancers are -methylcellulose, hydroxypropyl methylcellulose etc.

Viscosity enhancer	Maximum concentration
Hydroxyethyl cellulose	0.8
Hydroxyproplymethylcellulose	1.0
Methylcellulose	2.0
Polyvinyl alcohol	1.4
polyvinylpyrrolidone	1.7

LIST OF VISCOSITY ENHANCERS

Formulation of Eye Drops

Since eyes are the most sensitive part of the human body therefore the most important factor that should be kept in mind while preparing these formulations is "Sterility" of the preparation. Eye formulations have the following requirements –

- Active pharmaceutical ingredient (API) for its therapeutic actions.
- An excipient which can be both aqueous or non-aqueous and helps in transport of the API. Non- aqueous vehicles are rarely used because they can cause irritation in the eyes. Mineral oil and petroleum are used together as an excipient.
- A preservative like – pilocarpine, atropine sulphate etc which prevents the growth of different microorganisms and increases the shelf life of the preparation.
- An adjuvant which again adds on to the stability of the formulation. For example- antioxidants like ascorbic acid and sodium bisulphite. Besides this they also improve the viscosity and pH of the formulation.
- Chelating agents like disodium edentate.
- Wetting agents like polysorbate 80

Generally, when an ophthalmic preparation is made more than one preservative are used to ensure maximum stability and less side effects. Another important factor governing the formulations side effects is the condition of the patient's eye. A healthy eye is easily able to prevent any microbial growth because of the body's Immunol response but an eye with damaged epithelia is prone to microbes. To avoid damage of the internal eye, during intraocular studies the preservatives are not added.

Benzalkonium chloride (0.01% w/v)	Chlorhexidine acetate (0.01% w/v)	Phenylmercuric Nitrate (0.002% w/v)
Atropine sulphate	cocaine	Tetracaine
Carbachol	Cocaine and homatropine	Chloramphenicol
Cyclopentolate		Fluorescein
Homatropine		Hydrocortisone and neomycin
Hyoscine		Lachesine
Phenylephrine		Neomycin
Physostigmine		sulphacetamide

Preservatives suitable for specific Eye Drops

FORMULATION OF EYE OINTMENTS

For the formulation of normal ointments different bases like white soft paraffin, yellow soft paraffin, wool fat and liquid paraffin are generally used but since the eye is sensitive to different materials only yellow soft paraffin, wool fat and liquid paraffin are used as bases in the preparation of eye ointments specifically. The liquid paraffin reduces viscosity of the base so that it becomes easy to apply and the wool fat improves absorption.

Therefore, we can say that for the preparation of ophthalmic ointments, the type of base used is important. An ideal base is non-irritating, melts and gets easily absorbed at body temperature and is sterile.

FORMULATION OF EYE LOTIONS

Eye lotions are aqueous liquids which are used to wash the eye with large volumes of solution. They are undissolved and sterile in nature. For first aid purposes these lotions are used. One thing to keep in mind while making these formulations is that they can cause irritation in the eyes if normal sterile saline is not used.

An ideal eye lotion is iso-osmotic to lachrymal fluid, do not contain any preservative, sterile in nature and should have a normal Ph.

METHODS OF PREPARATION

Preparation of Eye drops:

- Dissolution and solution preparation -The active pharmaceutical ingredient (API) is added with the excipients and other adjuvants, preservatives, antioxidants, tonicity and viscosity enhancers etc.
- Clarification – It is the process in which we pass the prepared solution through different filters have minute pore size (0.40-1.20 micrometre). The clarified solution which comes out of these filters is transferred for sterilisation into containers or is kept in holding tanks for a few days before sterilization.
- Sterilization -In this process autoclaving is done at standard temperature i.e 121degree for 15 minutes or 115 degree for 30 minutes at a pressure of about 1.5 bar to 4.5 bar approximately. For dry heat sterilization which is performed for non-aqueous solutions heating at 160 degrees for 2 hours or at 180 degrees for one hour is required.
- The container after this is sealed properly.

Preparation of Eye ointment:

Yellow soft paraffin and wool fat are added together in a vessel kept in water bath and they are melted. After they completely melt the liquid paraffin is added. This mixture is then passed through a filter paper which is course in nature. Usually, Whitman 54 is used for the same. At last dry heat sterilization is performed at 160-degree temperature for 2 hours or at 180-degree temperature for 1 hour. The base is added, and packaging is done.

Preparation of Eye Lotion:

To the PW i.e purified water zinc sulphate and boric acid is added. This step is followed by filtration and transfer into a fluted bottle. This fluted bottle is sealed properly and autoclaved.

CONTAINERS

For making eye drops two types of containers that are -single and multiple dose containers are used. These containers should be made of such a material that do not absorb any part of the ophthalmic preparation and should not adsorb it as well. Along with this the material should be of such quality that it should not react with the preparation and most importantly should be sealed in a such a manner that no moisture from outside can destroy the preparation. It should not leach into the solution and should be sterilized properly before any amount of formulation is added.

Generally, these containers are made up of glass or plastic.

- Single dose container – Storage and precise dosing has been an issue in using multiple dose containers that are traditionally used, so single dose containers are better to use. These containers are made up of polypropylene having a nozzle at the top and a sealed base. In an outer heat-sealed pouch, they are autoclaved.
- Plastic bottles made up of polyethylene or polypropylene are used commercially. They are filled under aseptic conditions after being sterilized with ionizing radiations.
- Glass bottles -Two types of glass bottles each having its own quality can be used to put any eye drop preparation. They are -neutral glass and soda glass. The neutral glass can be autoclaved multiple times, but the latter can only be autoclaved once. These bottles are amber coloured so that no reaction takes place because of light getting in contact with the preparation.

Other parts of these container used in eye drops are – teats, flange, cap, rim, and dropper tube.

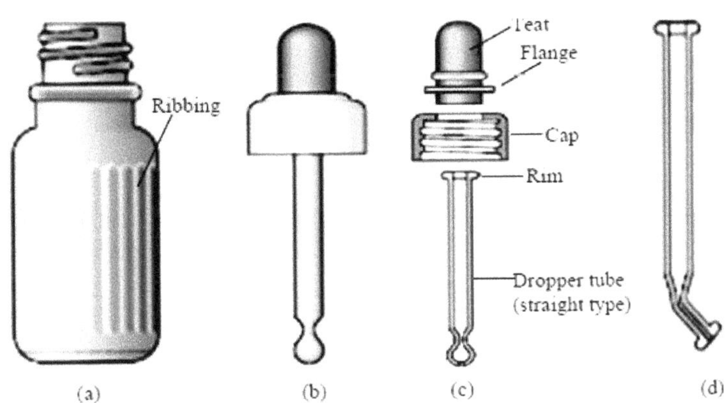

Eye Dropper Bottle a) Bottle b) Assembled Closure c) Components of closure d) Dropper Tube

Eye ointments are packed in tubes usually which are collapsible or made up of polyvinyl chloride. It can also be made a single dose container. The tube should be cleaned properly by-passing dust free air.

Eye lotions are filled in fluted coloured bottles and the top should be made of metal or plastic. The inner portion of such caps should also be made of the same so as to avoid microbial growth which otherwise can take place if cork is used instead.

LABELLING

An ophthalmic product's label should have the following information:

1) Name of the product,
2) Concentration and name of the API used,
3) Concentration and name of the adjuvants,

4) Volume of preparation present in the container,
5) Batch number
6) Date of expiration
7) Specific storage conditions and warnings related to the preparation if any,
8) Directions for use after opening the container,
9) Address and name of the manufacturer,
10) It should be specified that the preparation is sterile.

EVALUATION OF THE OPTHALMIC PREPARATIONS

There are certain parameters on which the ophthalmic preparations are evaluated, these are -sterility, uniformity of the dosage form, leachable and extractables, antimicrobial preservatives, container uniformity, closure integrity of the container, viscosity, antioxidant content, particle size distribution and resuspendibility.

Different tests are also performed to ensure the product quality. For example – test for minimum fall, test for metal particles, test for squeezability is performed for ophthalmic ointments; visual methods, light blockage method, coulter counter method, leak test, spark detector method is performed for ophthalmic injections.

- Sterility – Since any microbial growth can have lethal effects on the life of the patient therefore, maintenance of sterility is of the top priority. The preparations should meet the standard requirements as given in the SOPs. The container should be properly sterilized before filling and the seal used should be of good quality.
- Uniformity of the dosage form – A test is performed to check the content uniformity and weight variation.
- Leachable and extractable – The materials used in packaging should not hamper the product by interacting with it chemically, physically etc.
- Antimicrobial preservatives – The establishment of acceptance criteria for content of antimicrobial preservatives in multiple dose system is important. Usually, radionuclides which are microbicidal are present in these praparations.
- Container uniformity- In suspensions we see that slowly one phase starts to settle at the time of storage, so the container uniformity should be evaluated to maintain stability.
- Closure integrity of the container – The packaging should be done in such a way that no moisture could not enter inside and spoil the preparation.
- Viscosity – Ophthalmic preparations should have high viscosity so that amount of time the medicine stay on the cornea is more and the drug could easily interact with the eyes.
- Antioxidant content – With the help of impurity testing oxidative degradation of the drug can be tested and acceptance criteria for the same should be established according to the amount of antioxidants required to keep the preparation stable.
- Particle size and distribution – With the help of stability testing it can be evaluated that whether there will be any change in the particle size at different conditions. The drop size is also fixed for such preparations and is between 20-70 microlitre.
- Resuspendibility – The particles in a suspension should not form a cake which cannot get redispersed after shaking and therefore using different techniques this should be evaluated.

FORMULATION OF INJECTIONS

Oral administration of some drugs is not possible due to enzymatic actions, so they are given in the form of isotonic aqueous solutions having Ph close to the ph of the body i.e 7.4. The release of drugs given intramuscularly are dependent on several factors and can be managed by – increasing viscosity of the vehicle and complex formulation.

Injections are divided into two types according to the capacity of the container/pouch or the volume of solution filled. If the volume of solution is less than or equal to 100 ml than it is called small volume parentral(SVP) and the one which has a volume more than 100ml comes under large volume parentrals (LVP).

PH and tonicity considerations – When giving dose intramuscularly a high range of ph is tolerable i.e2-12 and it decreases as we reach subcutaneous layer. The main idea is to maintain the ratio of ph and stability; ph and solubilty and keeping the range near the ph of the body i.e 7.4.

Target osmolarity is 280-290 mosl/l and it should be isotonic with the human plasma.

Choice of excipients – The excipients are given to insure stability and efficacy and since the drugs should be isotonic to human plasma, in cases of hypotonicity they are added. They also decrease irritation of the eye.

FORMULATION OF STERILE POWDERS

Drugs which are unstable in the solution form but are still important in the pharmaceutical aspects are made as powders which are dry and solid. These are dissolved in water just before administration. Example – cefuroxime sterile powder. In the formulation of these sterile powders fillers or bulking agents, buffering agents, collapse temperature modifiers, tonicity modifiers (sodium chloride), antimicrobial agents (paraben, phenol), solubilizing agents (tweens) and complexing agents are used.

Example of fillers are – Mannitol, glucose, dextran etc and they are used to make up the volume of of cake.

Example of buffering agents – sodium citrate, sodium phosphate etc. They resist ph change.

Example of collapse temperature modifiers – gelatin and dextran. They increase the collapse time.

FORMULATION OF LARGE VOLUME PARENTRALS

LVPs are the single dose injections having container capacity of more than 100ml. Their composition includes – API, vehicle (solid, water, non-aqueous), tonicity adjusters like dextrose, buffers (glutamate), antioxidants, complexing agents etc. After the manufacturing of the LVPs which is done by mixing all the above constituents as decided by the industries the formulation is kept in a holding tank for a few days and then they are transferred to filling machines. This filling is done at very low temperatures and then sterilization step takes place in which the preparation is heated at 121 degrees for 30 minutes. The last step is packaging and storage.

FORMULATION OF LYOPHILIZED PRODUCTS

In lyophilization process removal of water is seen by freezing it at -50 degrees and then primary and secondary drying is done. Primary aim is to decrease the moisture content to inhibit microbial growth. While formulating lyophilized products excipient selection is important and the stability of the API should be known properly. Different types of excipients used are – bulking agents (mannitol), buffers, lyoprotectants and cryoprotectants (disaccharides, amino acids), tonicity modifiers (dextrose), others.

Lyoprotectants and cryoprotectants are drug stabilizers which protects the APIs and prevents its degradation.

REFERENCES

- *Dr. KL Senthilkumar (2019) Industrial Pharmacy. Thakur Publication.*
- *Chaitanya Sagar K. (2013) Formulation Development and Evaluation of Ophthalmic Solution of Timilol maleate 0.5 %, Tamil Nadu Dr. MGR Medical University*
- *Dr. B Prakash Rao (2019) Industrial Pharmacy. Nirali Publication.*
- *Leon Lechman and H. Lieberman (1990), Varghese Publishing house.*
- *Lubrizol Corporation, Lyophilization of complex drug Products : Formulation Challenges.*
- *ResearchGate (2018), Formulation and Evaluation of an injectable solution as a dosage form.*
- *Remixeducation (2021), Formulation of sterile powders, injections or lyophilized products.*
- *Dennis Jenke , An introduction to large volume parentrals (LVP) as a pharmaceutical dosage form and an E&L Challenge.*

CHAPTER IX

COSMETICS

Cosmetic as a product (excluding pure soap) is intended to be applied to the human body for cleansing, beautifying, promoting attractiveness, or altering the appearance. These are composed of chemical constituents that are either derived from natural, semisynthetic or synthetic sources. The word cosmetic refers to any substance or preparation that enhances the appearance of the face, hair or other bodily features.

Cosmeceuticals, a branch of cosmetics, are cosmetic products with bioactive ingredients aimed to having medical benefits. This name is an amalgamation of "cosmetics" and "pharmaceuticals".

Cosmetics are usually understood to represent only makeup products, for instance lipstick, eye shadow, foundation, mascara, blush, highlighter, bronzer, and several other products, but it also embodies toothpastes, shampoos, conditioners and hair dyes.

ADVANTAGES

- Enhances the skin
- Hydrates and clears the skin
- Easy to apply
- Contamination free
- Protects skin from dirt, pollution and harmful UV rays

DISADVANTAGES

- May cause allergic reactions
- Expensive
- Triggers Premature Aging
- May cause cancer or other deadly diseases
- Can lead to hormonal imbalance

An excipient is added to the formulation along with active pharmaceutical ingredient to increase the volume and enhance the physiochemical properties of the preparation. Some of the excipients used in the formulation of cosmetics are:

- Stiffening agents- The purpose of stiffening agent is to make the mixture firm.
- Colouring agents- These are organic or inorganic and soluble or insoluble colours that provide colour to the preparation.
- Opacifying agents- These are used to make the surface smooth and slippery.
- Softening mixtures increase the coverage proficiency by softening the lipstick.
- Preservatives help protect the preparation from microbes.
- Flavouring agents add flavour to the lipstick preparation.
- Perfumes provide mind-blowing aromas and essences.
- Emollient helps make the skin soft without any moisture.
- Humectants are the agents that soften the skin and have moisture in them.

- Abrasive and Polishing agents are those that help provide a smooth and reflecting surface.

- Detergents and Foaming Agents clean the surface and produce foam on activation.

- Binding Agents also known as binders assists clamp the preparation together.
- Sweetening agents are excipients that add sweet taste to the preparation.
- Emulsifier is an excipient that helps stabilize the preparation.
- Modifiers help alter the thickness and texture of the preparation.
- Wetting agents aid in reducing the surface tension and increase flowability.

In this chapter, we are going to learn formulation and preparation of the following cosmetic preparations.

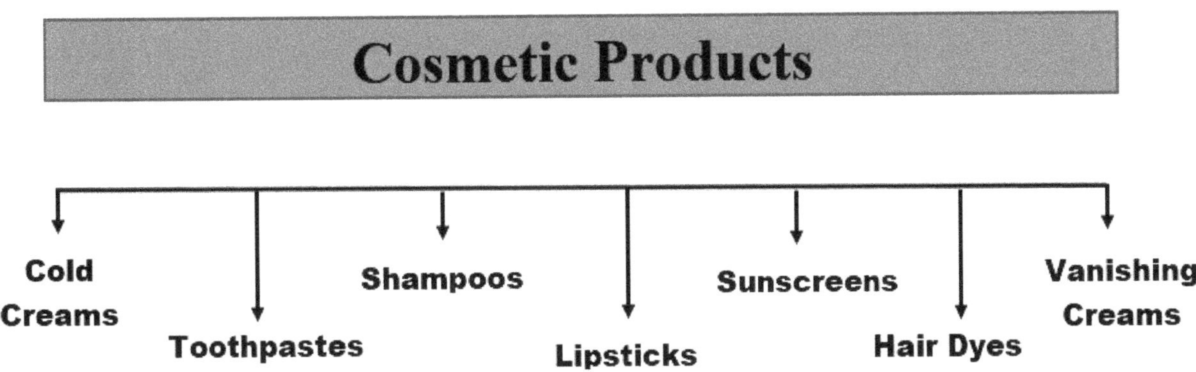

1. LIPSTICKS

Lipstick is a cosmetic formulation that is applied on the lips and gives a shiny, glossy, attractive and moist appearance. Lipstick may also be defined as the dispersion of tinting matter in a base consisting of a blend of oils, fats and waxes with different aromas and essences shaped in the form of sticks to apply.

Formulation of Lipsticks

The lipstick formulation is formed by blending oils and waxes in variable proportions in order to attain a desired viscosity and melting point.The formulation of lipstick consists of the following ingredients:

- Solid Mixture such as waxes.
- Liquid Mixtures such as oils, stearates, and water.
- Colouring Agents
- Opacifying Agents such as titanium dioxide.
- Softening Mixtures such as lanolin derivatives, cocoa butter, and petroleum.
- Preservatives
- Essence and Flavouring Agents comprise of oils such as peppermint oil, cinnamon oil, rose oil and several others.

Since the lipstick mass can be combined and kept for later use, the amalgam does not blend as soon as it is dispensed.

Table 1: Formulation Example for Quantity 100 g

Components	Quantity
Castor Oil (Dissolving Liquid)	27g
Bees Wax (Stiffening Agent)	20g
Ozokerite Wax (Increases Melting Point)	10g
Carnauba Wax (Provides Rigidity)	5.5g
Lanolin (Covering Agent/Emollient)	5g
Paraffin (Stiffening Agent)	3g
Isopropyl Myristate (Blending Agent)	3g
Acetyl Alcohol (Co-solvent)	2g
Propylene Glycol (Humectant)	11g
Propylene Glycol Monoricinoleate (Humectant)	4g
Eosin (Dye)	2.5g
Colour	10g
Rose Oil (Perfume)	q.s.
Paraben (Preservative)	q.s.
Tocopherol (Antioxidant)	q.s.

General method of preparation for Lipsticks

- The raw materials are melted and mixed in three different containers. First mixture contains solvents, second contains oils, and the third contains fats and waxy substances. These are heated.
- Then the solvent solution and liquid oil are blend with colour pigments. After the pigment batch is ready, it is mixed with hot wax. The mixture is agitated to release any air bubbles formed. Then, the mixture is transferred into tubing moulds, frozen and removed from the moulds.
- The mixture passes through a roller mill, crushing away the colourant to avoid the "grainy" sensation of the lipstick. This process allows air into the oil and pigment mixture. The mixture is stirred for numerous hours.
- After the pigment mass is powdered and mixed, it is added to the heated wax batch until a consistent colour is attained. The liquid lipstick can then be filtered and shaped, or it can be transferred into a container and stored for future moulding.

Evaluation of Lipsticks

a. Colour
b. Texture
c. pH
d. Melting point
e. Breaking point
f. Softening point
g. Surface anomalies
h. Stability

a. Rancidity
j. Microbial testing
k. Break Load test
ax. Skin Irritation test

2. TOOTHPASTES

A toothpaste is defined as a semi-solid preparation for removing naturally occurring deposits from teeth. It is used simultaneously with a toothbrush. The function of a toothpaste is to clean the teeth adequately, that is, to remove plaque, stains and food stuck between the spaces. It leaves the mouth with a cool and fresh sensation. The toothpaste must be harmless and convenient to use. Toothpaste is used to maintain health of teeth as well as the aesthetics value of the teeth. It also promotes oral hygiene.

Formulation of Tooth Paste

- Abrasive and Polishing Agents
- Detergents and Foaming Agents
- Humectants
- Binding Agents
- Sweetening Agents
- Flavouring Agents such as citral and lime juice.
- Preservatives
- Colours
- Miscellaneous Agents

- Anti-caries Agents prevent decaying of teeth
- Anti-bacterial Agents protect from microbes
- Desensitizing Agents diminish or eradicate the sensitivity.

Table 2: Formulation Example for Green Toothpaste

Components	Quantity
Turmeric Extract	5g
Aloe-vera Extracts	5g
Guava Extracts	5g
Neem Extracts	5g
Balsam Extracts	5g
Activated Charcoal	2g
Calcium Carbonate	4g
Gum Arabic	35g
Lime Juice	5ml
Coconut Oil	6ml
Mint Oil	6ml
Honey	20ml
Deionised Water	15ml

General Method of preparation for Toothpaste

i. The first and the foremost step is to weigh the ingredients and to ensure correct quantities have been taken. Then, the ingredients are blended in a stainless-steel vessel.
ii. Water and humectant are mixed first and then the other ingredients. The temperature and humidity are set. The mixing is keenly observed to ensure proper mixing of the ingredients.
iii. After the ingredients are mixed together, the finished amalgam obtained is transferred to a high-speed filling machine that pumps the paste into a tube through its open bottom.
iv. The end of the tube is sealed closed and pressed when the tube is filled with the paste.
v. The filled and pressed tubes are packed into different boxes and are out for retailing. The boxes are later put into master cartons and transported to distribution centres, stockrooms and stores.

Table 3: Composition of Toothpaste

Ingredient type	Typical %	Function
Liquid Base	White - 30 Gel - Up to 80	Polyols, most commonly sorbitol (glycerin is also used) act as a humectant, preventing the product from drying out and preserving the texture and flavor. Polyol solutions can contain up to 30% water; additional water (10-25%) completes the liquid base.
Fillers and Abrasives	White - 20-50 Gel - 15-25	Various ingredients provide the polishing action in white toothpastes; these include calcium carbonate, hydrated silica, sodium bicarbonate, dicalcium phosphate and sodium metaphosphate. In clear gel type products, hydrated silica is used to provide polishing and "body."
Rheology Modifiers	0.5-2	Used to obtain several properties: the toothpaste must flow easily but not too rapidly from the tube; it must "break" easily without being "stringy"; it must sit on the toothbrush without sinking in; these ingredients are also used to keep fillers/abrasives in suspension. Various ingredients are used, including CMC, carrageenan, xanthan gum and cellulose gum.
Detergent	0.5-2.5	Added to make the product foam when brushing. This helps dispersion and retention of the product in the mouth. SLS (Sodium Lauryl Sulphate) is most commonly used.
Active Ingredient	0.3	Fluoride can be added to help prevent tooth decay. Sodium fluoride, sodium monofluorophosphate and stannous fluoride are used, subject to legislation, etc.
Flavor	0.5-2	Flavoring is added to disguise the unpleasant taste of the detergent. It also provides "freshness." Typically mint (and sometimes menthol and cinnamon) flavoring oils are used.
Sweetener	0.2	Sweeteners include sodium saccharinate.
Coloring	0.1	Titanium dioxide can be added to white toothpaste as a coloring; gel toothpastes may be manufactured in a number of colors using food grade products.
Preservative	0.2	Sodium benzoate, ethyl paraben, methyl paraben.

3. CREAMS

Semisolid dosage forms that contain one or more drug elements dissolved or dispersed in an appropriate base are called creams. These creams are intended for external use only. Creams are classified into two categories on the basis of their emulsion type:

a. Water in Oil Type- Cold Creams
b. Oil in Water Type- Vanishing Creams

A. Cold Creams

- Cold creams are water in oil emulsions of fats and water that are used to clean, moisten and soften the skin.
- When applied on the skin, cold creams produce a cooling effect due to slow evaporation of water present in the emulsion.
- These are also used to remove makeup and can soften tough skin, for instance, in places like knees and elbows. It helps keep the skin protected from harsh weather conditions.
- Mostly, cold creams are prepared by a saponification reaction between beeswax and alkali borax.

Formulation of Cold Cream

- White Beeswax is the base of the cream.
- Mineral Oil used is liquid paraffin.
- Borax provides whiteness to the cream.
- Alcohol, glycerine and lanolin
- Fragrances are added for alluring aroma.
- Vehicle
- Preservatives

Table 3: Formulation Example for Cold Cream

Components	Quantity (%w/w)
Oil Phase	
Beeswax(Thickening Agent)	16
Mineral Oil	45.0
Aqueous Phase	
Borax(emulsifier)	1
Preservative	q.s
Perfume	q.s
Water	100

Method of preparation for Cold Creams

- Beeswax and liquid paraffin are taken in the required quantity, weighed and melted in a china dish by boiling in a water bath up to 70 °C.
- In another container, borax and water are heated at 70 °C.
- When both the oily phase and aqueous phase reach the same temperature, that is, 70 °C, borax solution is gradually added to the melted beeswax drop by drop.
- The mixture is constantly stirred until it cools down.
- When the temperature lowers down to 40-45 °C, we add rose oil and mix uniformly until a homogenous semi-solid mass is obtained.

A. **Vanishing Creams**

- Vanishing creams are creams that easily spread and disappear on application on the skin.
- These are composed of emollient esters which leave a thin apparent film on the skin.
- These are mainly composed of stearic acid.
- Stearic acids melts above body temperature and crystallizes in an invisible form providing a non-greasy layer. It also imparts an attractive appearance on the cream.

Formulation of Vanishing Cream

- Stearic acid
- Humectant
- Alkali
- Vehicle
- Aroma
- Preservative
- Emulsifier

Table 4: Formulation Example for Vanishing Creams

Components	**Quantity**
Oily Phase	
Stearic acid, triple pressed	15.0%
Acetyl alcohol (Emollient and emulsifier)	0.50%
Isopropyl myristate (non-greasy emollient)	3.00%
Aqueous Phase	
Sodium hydroxide (Alkali)	0.18%
Potassium hydroxide (Alkali)	0.50%
Glycerol (Humectant)	5.0%
Water (Vehicle)	75.82%
Perfume	q.s
Preservatives	q.s

Method of preparation of Vanishing Creams

- Stearic acid is melted in a china dish in a water bath.
- Dissolve potassium hydroxide, water and glycerine in a separate beaker and heat the solution to 70 °C on water bath.

- When both the aqueous phase and the oily phase reach the same temperature, the aqueous phase is added to the oily phase with constant stirring.
- The china dish is removed from the heat and stirred continuously. When the temperature reaches 40 °C, perfume is added and mixed uniformly until the mixture cools.
- A homogenous cream is obtained.

DIFFERENCE BETWEEN O/W AND W/O EMULSIONS

Oil in water emulsion (o/w)	Water in oil emulsion (w/o)
Water is the dispersion medium and oil is the dispersed phase	Oil is the dispersion medium and water is the dispersed phase
They are non greasy and easily removable from the skin surface	They are greasy and not water washable
They are used externally to provide cooling effect e.g. vanishing cream	They are used externally to prevent evaporation of moisture from the surface of skin e.g. Cold cream
Water soluble drugs are more quickly released from o/w emulsions	Oil soluble drugs are more quickly released from w/o emulsions
They are preferred for formulations meant for internal use as bitter taste of oils can be masked.	They are preferred for formulations meant for external use like creams.
O/W emulsions give a positive conductivity test as water is the external phase which is a good conductor of electricity.	W/O emulsions go not give a positive conductivity test as oil is the external phase which is a poor conductor of electricity.

Evaluation of Creams

Physical properties: The cream was observed for the color, odor and appearance.

Washability: The cream was applied on the hand and observed under the running.

pH: The pH meter was calibrated with the help of standard buffer solution. Weigh 0.5 gm of cream dissolved it in 50.0ml of distilled water and its p H was measured with the help of digital pH meter.

Viscosity: Viscosity of the cream was determined with the help of Brookfield viscometer at 100 rpm with the spindle no. 7.

Spread ability test : The cream sample was applied between the two glass slides and was compressed between the two-glass slide to uniform thickness by placing 100 gm of weight for 5 minutes then weight was added to the weighing pan. The time in which the upper glass slide moved over the lower slide was taken as a measure of spread ability.

Spread ability=m *l/t

m =weight tight to upper slide

l =length moved on the glass slide

t =time take

Irritancy test: Mark an area (1sq.cm) on the left-hand dorsal surface. The cream was applied to the specified area and time was noted. Irritancy, erythema, edema, was checked if any for regular intervals up to 24 hrs. and reported.

Test for microbial growth: Agar media was prepared then the formulated cream was inoculated on the plate's agar media by steak plate method and a controlled is prepared by omitting the cream. The plates were placed in the incubator and are incubated in 37 C for 24 hours. After the incubation period, the plates were taken out and the microbial growth were checked and compared with the control.

Saponification value: Take 2 gm of the substance and reflux it with the 25 ml of 0.5 N alcoholic KOH for 30 minutes. Then add 0.1 ml of phenolphthalein as a indicator and titrate it with the 0.5 N HCL.

Saponification value=(b-a) *28.05/W

a =volume of titrate

b =volume of titrate

w =weight of substances in gram

Acid value: Take 10 gm of the cream dissolved in accurately weighed in 50 ml mixture of the equal volume of alcohol and solvent ether. Then attached the flask with the condenser and reflux it with the slow heating until the sample gets completely dissolve then add 1 ml of phenolphthalein and titrate it with 0.1 N NaOH until it gets faint pink color appears after shaking in 20 seconds.

Acid value=n*5.61/w

w =weight of the substances

n =the number of ml in NaOH required.

Dye test: The scarlet red dye is mixed with the cream. Place a drop of the cream on a microscopic slide then covers it with a cover slip, and examines it under a microscope. If the disperse globules appear red the ground colorless. The cream is o/w type. The reverse condition occurs in w/o type cream i.e. the disperse globules appear colorless.

Homogeneity: Homogeneity was tested via the visual appearance and test.

4. HAIR DYES

Hair dyes are colouring agents that provide a different colour to your hair. Several reasons to colour hair include:

i. Colouring to have a new, attractive and fashionable look,
ii. To colour aging grey hair,
iii. To change colour for a temporary occasion.

There are 3 types of hair colour:

a. Temporary hair colour
b. Semi-permanent hair colour
c. Permanent hair colour

Formulation of Hair Dyes

- Modifiers
- Antioxidants
- Dyes
- Alkali
- Soaps
- Ammonia
- Wetting agents
- Fragrances

Table 5: Formulation Example for Hair Dyes

Components	Quantity
Quaternary ammonium compound (colour)	10-12g
Anionic surfactant	8-10g
Acid (buffer)	6-8g
Alkanolamide (surfactant)	4-6g
Dye stuff (colour)	1-2g
Water (solvent)	q.s. to 100ml

Method of preparation of Hair dyes

- The ingredients are checked and certified by the manufacturer in house.
- Then, the dye chemicals are accurately weighed and added to a tank, where water is piped in at 70 °C and the mix is agitated for 20 minutes.
- Pre-mix, such as surfactants, alkalis and solvents are added to the tank and blended thoroughly.

5. SUNSCREENS

Sunscreen is a photo protective preparation that absorbs or reflects the ultraviolet rays of the sun. They help protect the skin from sunburn, pre-mature aging and prevent skin cancer. Sunscreens are made in numerous forms, such as lotions, sprays, gels, foams, sticks, powders.

Classification of Sunscreens

a. **Physical Sunscreens-** Physical sunscreens are also known as inorganic sunscreens. These preparations reflect and scatter ultraviolet radiation due to large particle size. They are opaque in nature and create a whitening effect. Physical sunscreen creates a thick and heavy layer on application.

Formulation of Physical Sunscreens

- Titanium dioxide
- Talc, kaolin
- Zinc oxide
- Ferric chloride
- Ichthyol, red petroleum

b. **Chemical Sunscreens-** Chemical sunscreens are the preparations that absorb ultraviolet radiation due to small particle size and are also known as organic sunscreens. These preparations do not leave a white residue on the skin and contain one or more active ingredients.

Formulation of Chemical Sunscreens

- PABA, PABA esters
- Benzophenones
- Cinnamates
- Salicylates
- Di galloyl trioleate
- Anthranilates

Method of preparation of Sunscreen Lotion

- Heat water and dissolve borax in it.
- Add salicylate and stir continuously to dissolve.
- Blend the aroma and the alcohol and then add glycerine to it.
- Now, add the above glycerine solution to the methyl salicylate solution and continuously stir for dissolution.
- Filter the solution. A clear, matter free liquid is obtained.

Table 6: Formulation example for sunscreen lotion

Components	Quantity (%)
Methyl salicylate	9.0
Glycerine	3.0
Borax	2.0
Alcohol	15.0
Water	70.5
Perfume	0.5

S. No.	Ingredients	Use	Components (% w/w)
1	Cetosteryl alcohol	Emulsifier	5
2	Stearic acid	Emollient, Coemulsifier	2
3	Cetomacrogal-1000	Emulsifier	2
4	Cetyl alcohol	Emollient, Coemulsifier	1
5	Carbopol 940	Gelling agent	0.5
6	Disodium EDTA	Chelating Agents	0.02
7	Na Methyl Paraben	Preservative	0.3
8	Na Propyl Paraben	Preservative	0.06
9	Triethanolamine	Surface active agent	0.5
10	Purified Water	Vehicle	62
11	*Lutein ester*	Active ingredient	1
12	*M. oleifera* seed oil	Active ingredient	1
13	*M. oleifera* containing *Lutein* ester (1%)w/w	Active ingredients	1

6. SHAMPOOS

A shampoo is a cosmetic preparation of surfactant in a suitable form- powder, liquid or solid; that when used under specific conditions will remove grease, dirt and skin debris from the hair shaft and scalp without harming the consumer. Shampoos provide a shiny appearance and make the hair soft and silky.

There are various types of shampoos utilized for different purposes or by different types of people. They are:

a. Powder Shampoo
b. Liquid Shampoo
c. Lotion Shampoo
d. Cream Shampoo
e. Specialized Shampoo

Formulation of Shampoos

- Surfactants
- Conditioning agents
- Foam builders
- Viscosity modifiers
- Opacifying agents
- Aroma
- Preservatives

Table 7: Formulation Example for Shampoos

Components	Quantity
Sodium lauryl sulphate	40%
Sodium chloride	4%
Aroma	q.s
Colour	q.s
Preservatives	q.s
Water	100ml

Method of Preparation of Shampoos

- To the detergent, add water to make a detergent solution. Divide the solution obtained into two containers.
- In the first container, a secondary surfactant such as alkanolamide solution is added and stirred continuously. If the solution dries, heat to liquid form.
- To the second half, add a suitable amount of perfuming agent and dissolve it.
- The obtained perfume solution is then added to the alkanolamide solution.
- Colour and preservatives are separately dissolved in a sufficient volume of water. The obtained liquid is added to the main solution.
- The solution is mixed with gentle stirring. The volume of the solution is made up to 100 ml with the addition of sterile water.

Ingredient type	Typical %	Function
Water	50 - 60	Deionized water is used to ensure bacterial degradation is minimized.
Surfactants	depending on concentration	The main cleaning agent, surfactants also produce the foam, act as emulsifiers and wetting agents, and can contribute to viscosity. Some have conditioning properties. Many surfactants are available in several forms: at a concentration of around 25-30%, or in "high active" form (around 70% concentration). A mixture of products is normally used to obtain the desired balance of properties.
Conditioners	5 - 12	Traditionally fatty oils, alcohols and waxes e.g. lanolin derivatives were added to shampoos. Increasingly proteins or silicones are used. These contribute a variety of effects, for example, proteins can moisturize dry hair and increase the strength and volume of the hair; Silicones can reduce surfactant irritation, increase the density and stability of the foam and improve "combability."
Viscosity Modifiers	1 - 3	The traditional thickening agent, Sodium chloride (common salt), is still widely used, although it is less effective with some additives and surfactant systems. This has led to increasing use of various carbomers, cellulose polymers, compounds of gums (e.g. guar), and polyethylene glycol (PEG) based thickeners.
pH Adjuster Preservative Coloring Fragrance	1 - 3 <1 <1 <1	The pH is adjusted to between 5 - 6 by addition of citric acid. Additives are sometimes used to give a pearl effect to the product. This is often simply used to improve the appearance of products which cannot be made clear due to some ingredients. The coloring, fragrance and preservative are added to complete the formulation.

CHAPTER X

Pharmaceutical Aerosols

Introduction

Pharmaceutical aerosols mean fine particles of drug or medicine (either solid or liquid, or both) that are kept in a container under pressure and that are released as a fine spray when a button is pressed.

Packing of therapeutic active ingredients in a pressurized system. It contains one or more therapeutic active ingredients which upon actuation emit a fine dispersion of liquid/solid materials in a gaseous medium. It depends on the compression of aerosols.

ADVANTAGES

1. Doses can be expelled without contamination
2. They can be delivered to the affected area in a desired way.
3. Easy and rapid on set of action
4. Provides efficacy of a drug
5. It protects the drug from gastrointestinal tract degradation.
6. Stability is enhanced by these substances negatively affected by oxygen and or moisture

DISADVANTAGES

1. They are expensive
2. They can produce toxic reaction sometimes
3. Allergic in some cases
4. It can cause inflammability at times
5. Some propellants cause depletion of the ozone layer.

CLASSIFICATION

A. Two phase system (liquid/ gas)
B. Three phase system (liquid/ gas/ solid)
C. Compressed gas

COMPONENTS OF AEROSOLS

- Propellants
- Containers
- Valves and Actuator
- Product concentrate

PROPELLANTS

A propellant is a substance used in the form of a pressurized gas to produce energy which is then used to create the motion of a fluid. There are several types of propellants that can be used to create pressure inside the tin.

Types of propellants

1. **Carbon Dioxide (CO2) Propellants**

Carbon dioxide is an ideal gas because it comes from natural gas. It is easily available from underground sources.

Pros :- a) It is inflammable in nature

b) It doesn't explode

c) CO2 propellant is non- flammable

Cons :- It is incompatible with water or traces of water in an aerosol tin.

1. **Chloro Fluoro Carbon (CHF)**

Desirable propellant for oral and inhalation purposes
Pros: a) Lack of toxicity
b) It is Inert in nature
c) The chances of an explosion are quite low.
d) CHF propellants are non- combustible
Cons: a) It contributes to depletion of the ozone layer
b) CHF propellants are expensive

CONTAINERS

They are 130 °F, but must be able to withstand high pressures ranging from 140 to 180 psig.

Ideal characteristics: Its adaptability to production methods

- Compatibility with formulation components
- Ability to maintain desired pressure for the product
- Interest in design
- It should be Cost effective

Metals

a) Aluminum containers are manufactured by an impact extrusion process; lighter in weight, less fragile, less incombustibility, greater resistance to corrosion due to its seamless nature. Pure water in pure ethanol causes corrosion in aluminum containers and organic resistance can be achieved by coating the inside of the container with Phenolic vinyl or epoxy and polyamide resins.

b) Stainless steel is generally used for inhalation of aerosols. There is no need for internal coating, a strong structure but avoided due to the high coast.

Glass containers

a) Uncoated glass containers have low cost, high clarity and contents can be seen at all times.

b) Plastic coated glass containers are protected by a plastic coating that prevents cracking of the glass in case of breakage.

VALVES

Modern day aerosols valves are multifunctional which dispense product in desired form as well as in measured quantity whenever required.

Types of valves

1. Continuous spray valves
2. Metering valves

Continuous spray valves are used for topical aerosols.

It consists of-

Ferrule or mounting cup: used to enclose volume in a container made of tin plated steel, Al, brass under a wall cup single or double coated with epoxy or vinyl resins.

Valve body or housing: It is built with nylon or delrin and opens at the point of attachment of the dip tube.

Stem: made from nylon or delrin, but metals such as brass and stainless steel may be used. When the stem is pressed, the product is discharged from the container.

Gasket: Buna-N and neoprene rubber are frequently used for gasket materials and are well-suited to most pharmaceutical formulations.

Dip tube: It is made up of polyethylene or polypropylene having a diameter between 3 to 3.2 mm. It gets formulation from the container up to the valve.

Metering valves distribute a portion of the liquid phase of preparation to be reproduced in which medicament is dissolved or dispersed.

It works on the principle of a chamber whose size determines the amount of medicine.

About 50 to 150 mg of fluid can be dispensed at a time using such a valve.

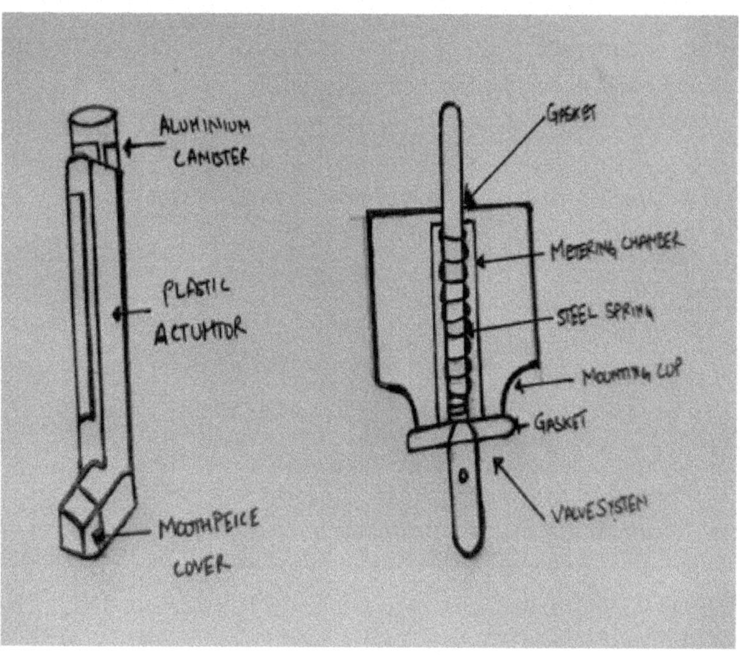

ACTUATORS

This allows for easy opening and closing of valves. The design of the actuator determines the proper and desired form of the aerosol product.

Types of Actuators

Spray actuators: These actuators are capable of breaking a stream into fine particles mechanically by rotating it through the various channels built into the container.

It can be used for topical preparations such as antiseptics, local anesthetics, and spray-on bandages.

Foam actuators: It comprises a large orifice which ranges from 0.070 to 0.125 inch.

Solid steam actuators: It allows passage of semi solid products such as ointments.

Special actuators: It transports the medicine to the appropriate site of action like throat, nose, dental, eyes etc.

Product concentrate

The release of air causes a sudden drop in air pressure inside the tin

The air inside the top of the tin is under a higher pressure than the air in the tube, so it pushes down on the product concentrate.

The focus of the product is compared to forcing the tube towards the mechanism for release.

The product concentrate comes out in the form of spray.

FORMULATION OF AEROSOLS

An aerosol formulation has two essential components, i.e.

Product concentrates contain active ingredients, or a mixture of active ingredients, and other essential agents such as solvents, antioxidants, and surfactants.

The propellant may be a single propellant or a mixture of different propellants.

Depending on the type of aerosol system used, pharmaceutical aerosols may be described as a fine mist, wet spray, quick-breaking foam, stationary foam, semi-solid, or solid can be extracted. The type of system selected depends on several factors, including the following: the physical, chemical and pharmacological properties of the active ingredients, and the site of application.

Type of systems-

1. Solution system

This system is also known as a two phase system. It consists of vapor and liquid phases. Depending on the type of spray required, the propellant may consist of a 50:50 ratio of propellant 12 or A-70 (which produces very fine particles), or propellant 12 and other propellants such as propellant 12/11, which produces 37.4 psig. With 1.412 g/ ml (density) at 70 °F. As other propellants with a vapor pressure lower than propellant 12 are added to propellant 12, the system pressure is reduced, resulting in the production of larger particles.

These sprays are also useful for topical preparations, as they cover the affected area with a film of active ingredients.

Table 2: Hydrocarbon in topical aerosols pharmaceutical preparation

Active Ingredients	Weight %
Active ingredient	up to 10 -15
Ethanol	up to 10 -15
Water	10 – 15
Hydro carbon propellant (A- 46)	55 – 70

2. Water based system

Relatively large amounts of water can be used to replace all or some of the non-aqueous solvents used in aerosols. Depending on the formulation, they are excreted in the form of a spray or a foam. To produce a spray, the formulation consists of active ingredients and solvents in animals and system in which the propellant is in the external phase. In this way, when the product is dispensed, the propellant vaporizes and disperses the active ingredients into fine particles. Since the propellant and water are not miscible, three-phase aerosols form (propellant phase, water phase and vapor phase). Ethanol has been used as a co-solvent to dissolve some propellants in water. Due to its surface tension-reducing properties, ethanol also aids in the production of smaller particles.

Surfactants have been used extensively to produce a suitable homogeneous dispersion, with approximately 0.5 to 2% surfactants being used. The propellant content varies from 25-60%, but can be as low as 5% depending upon the nature of the product. In order to achieve the desired fine particle size with products containing large amounts of water and low ratios of propellant, a mechanical breakup actuator with a "vapor tap valve" must be used.

3. Suspension or dispersion system

This system has been developed primarily for use with oral inhalation. This system involves the dispersion of active ingredients in a propellant or mixture of propellants. In order to reduce the settling rate of the dispersed particles, various surfactants or suspending agents have been added to the system.

Table 3: Formulation using epinephrine bitartrate

Active Ingredients	Weight/Volume %
Epinephrine Bitartrate (within 1 to 5 microns)	0.5
Sorbitan Trioleate	0.50
Propellant 114	49.50
Propellant 12	49.50

Epinephrine bitartrate has minimal solubility in the propellant system, but is sufficiently soluble in fluids in the lungs to exert therapeutic activity.

4. Foam system

Emulsions and foam aerosols contain active ingredients, aqueous or non-aqueous vehicles, surfactants and propellants, and are delivered as a stable or quick-breaking foam depending on the nature and composition of the material.

A. **Aqueous Stable Foam**

Table 4: Formulation of aqueous stable foam

Active Ingredients	Weight/Weight %
Oil waxes	95 – 96.5
O/w surfactants	95 – 96.5
Water	95 – 96.5
Hydrocarbon propellant	3.5 – 5

While the total propellant content can be up to 5% in some cases, it is usually around 8-10% v/v or 3 or 5% w/w. As the amount of propellant A-70, A-46, etc. increases, a harder and drier foam is produced. Low propellant concentration leads to wet foam.

B. Non aqueous Stable Foams

Table 5: Formulation of non- aqueous stable foam

The emulsifying agents found to be most effective were, for example, from the class of glycol esters. Propylene Glycol Monostearate.

C. Quick-Breaking Foams

In this system, the propellant is in the outer stage. When delivered, the product is oozed as a foam, which then breakdowns into a liquid.

Table 6: Formulation of quick- breaking foams

Active Ingredients	Weight/Weight %
Ethyl alcohol	46.0 – 66.0
Surfactants	0.5 -5.0
Water	28.0 – 42.0
Hydrocarbon propellant	3.0 – 15.0

The surfactant can be of non- ionic, anionic, or cation type. It should be soluble in all kinds of solvents. If the proportions of the ingredients are varied, foams with a wide range in consistency can be obtained.

5. **Thermal Foam**

It is used to make hot foam for shaving. However, they were not readily accepted by the consumer, and were soon discontinued due to the inconvenience of use, expense and lack of effectiveness. The same technique was used to remove hair dyes and dyes. Corrosion problems, and therefore failed. Suitable for distribution in medicinal foam in which the application of heat would be suitable pleasant.

6. Intranasal Aerosol

Targeted drug delivery systems for drug deposition in the nasal passages have long been used as the most effective means of administering drugs for the purpose of producing local or systemic effects. More recently, methods of administering intranasal preparations have been limited to nasal drops, non-pressurized nasal sprays (gauze), inhalants, and intranasal gels, creams, and ointments. A newer option is pressurized metered nasal aerosols.

MANUFACTURING OF AEROSOLS

It requires quality control measures during the filling operation to ensure that both the concentrate and the propellant should be brought together in proper proportion. The aerosol concentrate is prepared and the sample is tested (early detection averts loss of other components). Once the propellant is added, the product is sealed in a container with a valve.

Cold filling method

This method requires cooling of all components, including the concentrate and propellant, to a temperature of -30 °F or 40 °F.

It consists of an insulated box fitted with copper tubing and the tubing is said to increase the area exposed to cooling. The insulated box should be filled with dry ice or acetone before use. Hydrocarbon propellants cannot be filled into aerosol containers using this apparatus because large amount of propellants are released and vaporized.

This can lead to the formation of an explosive mixture.

Procedure- The product concentrate is refrigerated to -40 °F and added to the cooled container, then the refrigerant propellant is added. A valve is then crumpled. The container passed through a hot water bath with the contender heated to 130 °F.

Limitation- This method is highly confined to non –aqueous products. The products which are adversely affected by high temperatures cannot be filled by this method.

Pressure filling method

It consists of a pressure burette that is capable of delivering small volumes of liquefied gas into an aerosol container under pressure. The propellant is added through an inlet valve located below or above the pressure burette. The propellant is allowed to flow through the aerosol valve into the container at its own vapor pressure. The trapped air exits through the upper valve. When the pressure of the burette and the vessel becomes equal, the propellant stops flowing. If propellant is to be added, then a hose leading to a cylinder of nitrogen is added to the upper valve. The pressure exerted by the nitrogen helps the propellant to flow into the container.

Procedure- The concentrate is added to the container at room temperature, the valve is crimped. A propellants are added below the cap. As the valve opening is tremendously small, this step takes time and bounds production. With the development of rotary filling machines that allow propellers to be added through and around the valve stem, there has been an increase in speed.

Compressed gas filling method

Compressed gases have high pressure and therefore require a pressure reducing valve. The equipment consists of a delivery gauge, a flexible hose pipe with a stand that can hold up to 150 pounds per square inch of mist pressure attached to a delivery gauge with a filing head.

Procedure- The product concentrate is filled into the container. The valve is placed and pressed onto the container. The air is removed from the container with the help of a vacuum pump. The filling head is inserted into the valve opening and the valve is depressurized and the gas is allowed to flow into the container. If the delivery pressure and the pressure inside the container become equal, the gas flow stops. Carbon dioxide and nitrous oxide are used when gas is needed in large quantities. The high solubility of the gas in the product can be achieved by moving the container manually or with the aid of mechanical shakers.

QUALITY CONTROL

It incorporates tests of-

PROPELLANTS

Propellants are with specification sheet.

Table 7: Specification sheet

PARAMETER	TESTED BY
Identification	Gas Chromatography
Purity	Moisture, Halogen, Non Volatile Residue Determination

CONTAINERS

Quality control aspects include the degree of conductivity of electric current as a measure of the exposed metals. The containers are checked for defects in the lining.

VALVES, ACTUATORS & DIPTUBES

The purpose of this test is to determine the magnitude of valve distribution & the degree of uniformity between individual valves.

Test solutions-

Table 8: Test solutions

Ingredients % w/w	Test Solutions A	Test Solutions B	Test Solutions C
Iso Propyl Myristate	0.10%	0.10%	0.10%
Dichloro Difluoro methane	49.95%	25.0%	50.25%
Dichloro tetrafluoro ethane	49.95%	25.0%	24.75%
Trichloro monofluoro methane	_	_	24.9%
Alcohol USP	_	49.9%	_
Specific Gravity @ 25* C	1.384	1.092	1.368

Procedure- Take 25 valves and place them on containers filled with specific test solutions.

Actuator with 0.020 inch orifice attached, temperature -25+_1°C. The valve is fully activated for 2 seconds and weighed. Again, the valve was activated for 2 sec and the difference between them represents the distribution in mg. Repeat this for a total of two separate deliveries for each of the 25 test units.

WEIGHT CHECKING

The weight is checked occasionally by inserting tarred empty aerosol containers into the filling line, which are removed from the concentrate and weighed. The same procedure is used to check the weight of the propellants.

LEAK TESTING

It is a means of checking and detecting valve spasm. Damaged containers due to leakage. This is done by measuring and comparing the amplitude of the crimp. The final test of valve closure is carried out by passing the filled containers through a water bath.

SPRAY TESTING

It serves to clean the dip tube of pure propellant and pure concentrate.

Checking for defects in valves and spray patterns.

EVALUATION OF AEROSOLS

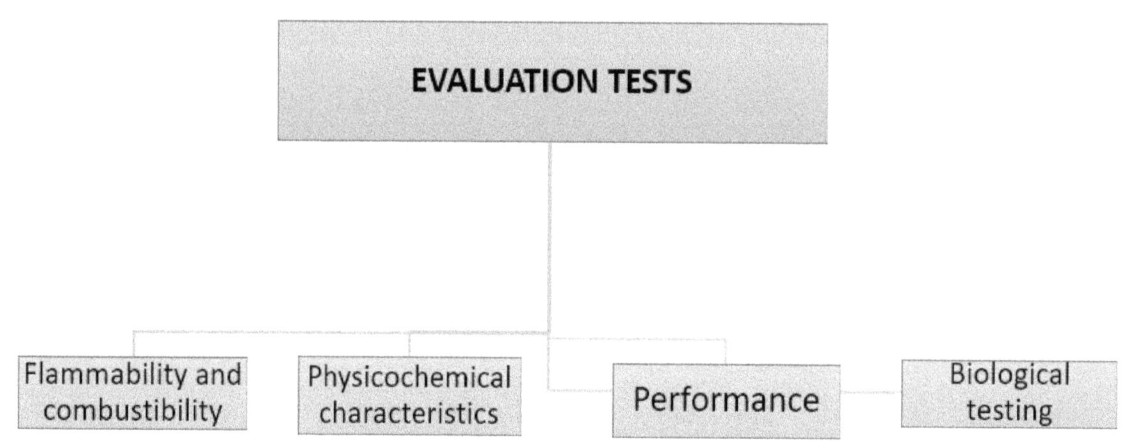

Flammability and combustibility

a. Flash point-

Apparatus: Tag Open Cup Apparatus

The product is then cooled to -25 °F and the test liquid temperature is allowed to rise gently and the temperature at which the vapor ignites is called the flash point.

b. Flame Projection-

The product is sprayed on a flame for 4 seconds and the flame is raised, the precise length is measured with a ruler.

Physicochemical characteristics

Table 9: Physiochemical properties of Aerosols

PROPERTY	METHOD
Vapor pressure	Can Puncturing Device
Density	Hydrometer
Moisture content	Karl Fisher Method Gas Chromatography
Identification of Propellants	Gas Chromatography IR Spectroscopy

Performance

a. Aerosol valve discharge rate

The aerosol product of proven weight is discharged for a specific amount of time.

By re-weighing the container, the weight changes. Is the discharge rate in g/sec per delivery time.

b. Spray pattern

In this method, the spray is unpigmented on the sheet which is treated with Dye-Talc mixture.

c. Dosage with metered valves

Reproducibility of prescribed dosage by:

Assay

Accurately weighing the filled container and then giving multiple doses. The containers were then weighed and separated. The distribution of the dose divided by the number in the mass gives the average dose.

d. Net Contents

Tared cans are placed on filling lines, reweigh & then difference in weight. is equal to net content.

In the destructive method: open the container and remove the content.

e. Foam stability

- Visual Evaluation
- Rotational Viscometer
- Penetration time of the foam for a given mass
- The time of the fall of the given rod which is put in the foam

f. Particle Size Determination

Cascade Impactor- A stream of particles propelled through a series of nozzles and glass slides at high velocity, with larger particles impacted at the low velocity stage, and smaller ones at the high velocity stage.

Light Scattering Decay- aerosol settles under the blustery conditions, the changes in the light of a Tyndall beam are measured.

Biological testing

a. Therapeutic Activity

Inhalation aerosols depend upon the particle size.

For topical aerosols, adsorption of therapeutic ingredient is checked and smeared on test areas.

b. Toxicity

For Inhalation Aerosols- exposing test animals to vapor sprayed from an aerosol container.

For Tropical Aerosols- irritation & chilling effects are determined.

CHAPTER XI

PACKAGING MATERIALS SCIENCE

Introduction

Packaging is the process by which pharmaceuticals are appositely packaged so that they retain their therapeutic effectiveness from the time of packaging to consumption. Packaging can be described as an art and science that involves preparing articles for transportation, storage, display and use. Pharmaceutical packaging is a measure of providing protection, presentation, identification, information and convenience to encourage compliance with a course of medicine.

Ideal characteristics

- The product should not be reactive
- They need to be non-toxic
- They should convene the applicable temper-resistance requirements
- They must protect the preparation from environmental ailments
- They have to be approved by the FDA
- They must be compatible with the high speed packaging equipment commonly employed
- They should not cause product degradation

TYPES OF PACKAGING

Primary: is the material which initially shrouds the product. This is the base package with an emphasis on both usability and appearance.Its objective is to identify, acquire product knowledge and assist in the consumption of the product.

For example- containers, ampules, dosing droppers, vials, syringes, blister packaging

Secondary: Its main use is to group individual units of a product and distribute large quantities of that product at the place of sale. It combines small product units into a single pack and assists in inventory management.

Example- boards, cartoons, box,

Tertiary: also known as bulk or transit packaging, used to transport products in bulk.

Example- barrel, containers

PACKAGING MATERIAL SELECTION

Physical form

Form of the product such as solid, liquid, semi solid or gaseous dosage forms.

Route of administration

Such as oral, parenteral, external etc.

Stability

Fluctuation in pressure, temperature, oxygen, moisture may adverse effects on the product.

Facilities available

Such as pressurized dispenser requires special filling equipment.

Contents

The product may react with the package, such as release of alkali from the glass or corrosion of metals and, in turn, affect the product.

Cost of product

Expensive products requires expensive packaging.

PACKAGING MATERIALS

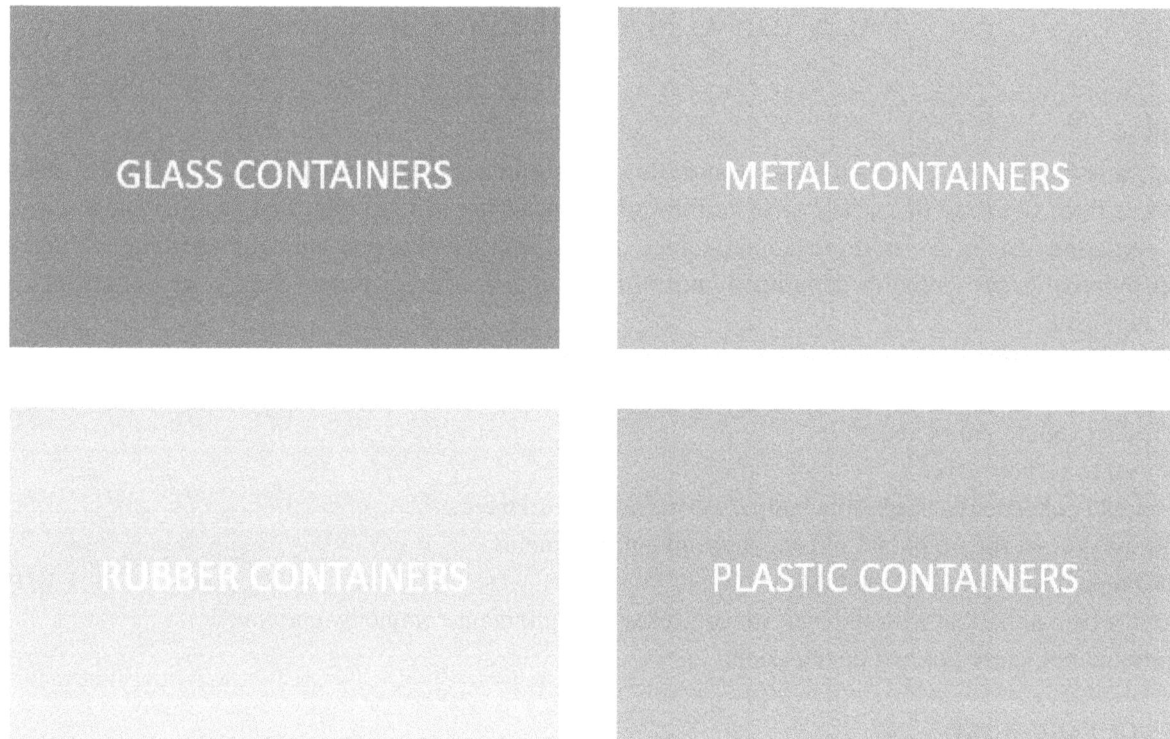

GLASS CONTAINERS

Glass has been broadly used as a pharmaceutical packaging material. It consists of sand, soda ash, limestone, cullet, aluminum, boron, potassium, magnesium, zinc, barium.

Advantages: • It is inert to most medicinal products.
• It is resistant to air and moisture.
• It allows easy inspection of the container's contents as it is transparent.
• The content can be protected from harmful rays by colored glass.
• They are pocket- friendly
• It is moldable in variously shaped containers.

Disadvantages: • Fragile (it is easily broken): Glass shatters and fractures.
• Costlier than plastic.
• As it is heavy, transport is expensive.
• In the content, alkali is released by certain glasses.

Types of glass

1. Type-I glass
2. Type-II glass
3. Type-III glass

1. **Type-I glass:**

Composition- Neutral glass, borosilicate glass, silicon dioxide and boron oxide.
Advantages- this glass has high endurance

- It has least reactivity
- Generally, ampoules and vials are made from type-I glass.
- It can defy strong acids, alkalis and all kinds of solvents. Lowered leaching action.

Uses- It is used for injections and water for injection.
- Appropriate for filling pharmaceutical formulations.

1. **Type-II glass:**

Composition- it is treated with soda lime. Soda (Na_2CO_3) is utilized to lower the glass conversion warmth of silica. In spite of this, soda increases the water solubility of silica. Hence, lime i.e. calcium oxide is utilized to increase the hydrolytic resistance.

Advantages- This glass has a lower melting point compared to Type I glass. Therefore, making is easy to manufacture and subsequently cheaper.

- It generates high hydrolytic resistance due to the surface treatment.

Uses- packaging of aqueous formulation
- Unlike other types of glass (types II and III), this type has a small amount of basic oxides, so it is used to pack solutions that can dissolve basic oxides in the glass.

3. **Type-III glass:**

Composition- silicon dioxide, soda ash, limestone is usually referred to as soda lime glass but it is untreated soda lime.

Uses- Provides only adequate resistance to leaching and is

Commonly used to produce dispensary metric medical bottles. It is also suitable for packaging of non-aqueous parenteral products and powders for injection.

PLASTIC CONTAINERS

Plastics in packaging have proven useful for a number of reasons, including the ease of use from which they can be made, their high quality, and the freedom of design for which they can be changed. Minimizing wear and tear at all levels of distribution and use, as well as to consumers. Plastic containers contain one or more polymers with some additives.

The amount and nature of the additive is determined by the nature of the polymer. In general, additives may include antioxidants, antistatic agents,

Dyes, opact modifiers, lubricants, plasticizers and stabilizers.

Advantages- Plastic containers are extremely resistant to breakage, thus providing protection.

- Flexible convenience product delivery
- It is suitable for use in container closure and as a secondary packaging.
- Easily affordable
- Light in weight and flexible

Disadvantages- additives in plastics easily dissolve in the product.

- Some plastics are sensitive to heat
- They are not chemically inert like type-I glass

All are to some extent permeable to moisture, oxygen, carbon dioxide etc. and most of the electrostatic attraction allows the repetition of light rays and less pigmented, black etc.

Types of plastics:

1. Thermoplastics
2. Thermosets

1. Thermoplastics-

On heating, it softens into a viscous liquid, which hardens again on cooling. Resistant to breakage and to provide cheap and perfect plastic to produce, attractive containers are chosen while providing the required protection to the product.

Example: polyethylene, PVC, polyamide, polycarbonate

2. Thermosets-

They can be malleable on heating but they do not become liquid. During heating, such a material forms permanent cross links between linear chains, resulting in solidification and damaging plastic flow.

For example: polyurethanes, urea formaldehyde, nylon, Polycarbonate Acrylonitrile butadiene styrene.

Plastics used for packaging:

Polyethylene

The density of polyethylene, which ranges from 0.91 to 0.96, directly determines the blow-molded container.

Advantages- • It is a good barrier against moisture but somewhat poor against oxygen and other gases.

• Most solvents do not attack polyethylene, and it is unaltered by strong acids
and alkali.

• Polyethylene provides ultimate protection for the largest of all its variations.
Number of products at minimum cost.

Disadvantages- lack of clarity in containers

• Relatively high rates of permeation of essential odors, tastes, and oxygen influence. Against the use of polyethylene as a container material for some pharmaceutical preparation.

Polypropylene

Polypropylene (PP) has recently gained the spotlight due to its remarkable features.

Advantages- its high melting point makes it appropriate for boiling packages and sterilizing products.

- Exceptional resistance towards strong acids and alkalis.
- Polypropylene does not stress- crack under any circumstances.
- It is an first-rate gas and vapor barrier

Disadvantages- it is fragile at low temperature

- In this unadulterated form, it is quite delicate at 0 °C and must be mixed with polyethylene or other materials to give the required impact resistance for packaging.

Poly-Vinyl Chloride (PVC)

It is the third most widely produced synthetic polymer of plastic.

Advantages- it preserves odor and is an excellent barrier to oxygen, moisture and gases.

PVC is unaffected by acids or alkalis apart from some oxidizing acids.

- It is pocket- friendly and clear material that is easily processed.

Disadvantages- PVC turns yellow when exposed to heat or ultraviolet light, unless the stabilizer is included by the resin supplier.

- If overheated, it begins to deform at 280 °F and the degradation products are extremely corrosive.
- In the manufacture of PVC compounds with calcium-zinc stabilizing materials, all ingredients are used in concentrations less than their maximum extractable concentration.

Polymonochloro-Trifluoroethylene (PCTFE)

It comes under market name ACLAR

Advantages- Permeability to moisture is quite low

- It is one of the utmost inert plastic.
- Newer homo polymers Rx 160, ultRx 2000 and 3000, SupRx 900 offer some benefits on copolymers with a low cost.

Disadvantages- The basic monomer chlorofluoroethylene C,C 1/73, is linked with toxicity.

- PCTFE is a good barrier against moisture, but a poor against O2, N2 and CO2 comparatively for PVdC.

Drug-Plastic Consideration

Drug-plastic considerations have been divided into the following:

1. Permeation
2. Leaching
3. Sorption
4. Chemical reaction and
5. Alteration in the physical properties of plastics or products.

1. Permeation:

The diffusion of gases, vapors or liquids through plastic packaging materials may adversely affect the shelf life of the drug.

For example, penicillin tablets were found to degrade in polystyrene containers, allowing water vapor to enter.

2. Leaching:

Most plastics contain a small amount of material to stabilize or provide a distinguishing property for plastics. The possibility of leaching or migration from a container exists for the pharmaceutical product. Problems can occur with plastics when dyed, relatively small amounts are added to the formula. Special colors can migrate to parenteral solution and cause toxic effects.

3. Sorption:

This process involves removing agents from the pharmaceutical structure by means of packaging material. Sorption can have serious consequences for pharmaceutical formulations containing important ingredients in the solution. Because high potency drugs are administered in low doses, the loss of sorption can significantly affect the therapeutic effectiveness of the formulation. In practice, the loss of preservatives is often a trouble. These agents act in low concentrations, which must be high enough to prevent the product from being protected from microbial growth.

4. Chemical reactivity:

Other materials used in the plastic composition may respond to one or more of the chemicals in the drug product. Sometimes the material of manufacture can be touched by plastic, even the little things. Non-chemical substances can change the appearance of plastics or pharmaceutical products.

5. Alteration in the Physical Properties of Plastics or Products:

The physical and chemical changes in packaging materials due to pharmaceuticals are called corrections. Pharmacological events like sorption, adsorption, and leaching may also play a role in changing the properties of plastics and causing their degradation. Deformation of polyethylene containers is often caused by diffusion of gases and vapor from the environment, or loss of material from the walls of the container.

METAL

It is commonly used to manufacture containers and for non- parenteral preparations

Advantages- They are resistant to light, moisture and gases.

- Form an outstanding tamper evident containers.
- They are made by impact extrusion into rigid and indestructible containers.

Disadvantages- They react with a few chemicals

- They are costly

TYPES OF METALS

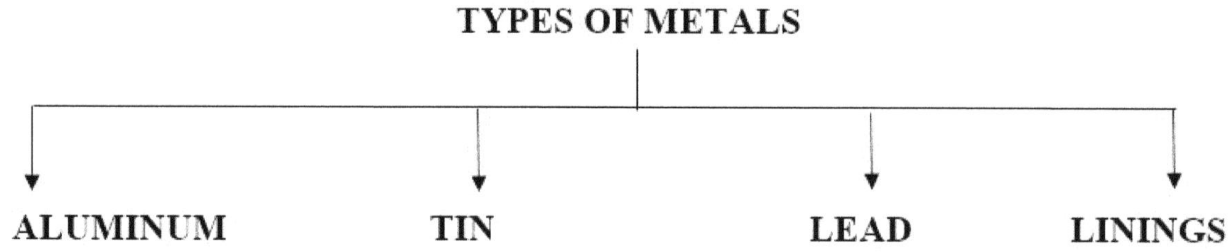

Tin

Tin containers are preferred for food, pharmaceuticals and any product which is considered to be sacred. It is the highly inert of all inflatable metal tubes.

Aluminum

It is an excellent barricade to light and chemicals. Aluminum tubes offer considerable savings in product shipping costs due to their weight. Impermeable and easy to work with in various formats depending on its thickness.

The densest aluminum is used for rigid containers such as aerosol cans and tubes for aerated tablets.

Intermediate thickness is when mechanical integrity is still important, but the pack must be able to perform under proper force. Example- semi solid preparation or collapsible tubes to roll over screw caps.

The thinnest aluminum is used in flexible foils, which are usually a component of laminated packing materials.

Lead

Lead has the lowest cost of all tube metals and is commonly used for non-food products such as adhesives, inks, paints and lubricants. It should not be used alone for anything taken internally because its exposure leads to lead poison. With the inner lining, lead tubes are used for products such as chloride tooth Paste.

Linings

If the product is incompatible with their metal, the interior can be flushed with a wax type composition or resin solution, although the lacquer causes are usually sprayed. A tube with epoxy lined costs about 25% more than the same tube. Wax linings are often used with water-based products in tin tubes and phenolic, epoxides and vinyl's are used with aluminum tubes which guard better than wax but at a higher cost.

RUBBERS

Rubber is mainly used for the manufacture of closures for vials, transfusion liquids, in the form of bottles, dropper bottles and washers in many other product types.

1. Natural rubbers

Suitable for multiple use closures for injectable products such as rubber after multiple needle insertions.

Disadvantages- it does not tolerate brittleness of multiple autoclaving well and leads to relative degrees of extractable material in the presence of additives.

- The risk of the product being absorbed into or on the rubber.
- It has a certain degree of moisture and gas permeability.

2. Synthetic rubbers

It contains fewer additives and thus less extractable and the product experiences less adsorption of the ingredients. Needles are less suitable for frequent insertion because they tend to push smaller rubber particles into the product fragments or cores. For example, silicone, butyl etc.

TAMPER RESISTANT PACKAGING

FIBROUS MATERIALS

Fibrous materials are an essential part of pharmaceutical packaging.

It includes: Labels, Cartons, Papers, Bags etc.

Application- It provides protection to things such as metal collapsible tubes.

Fiberboard outers, either as solid or corrugated board, also find considerable application for bulk shipments.

Provides better stacking for display of stock commodities.

FILMS, FOILS & LAMINATES

- Manufactured using cold- molding packaging machines
- Capsules, pills, tablets etc. are packed in these
- No breaking, delamination or pinholes
- It has excellent barrier properties, effectually protecting the drugs from water vapor, oxygen and ultraviolet
- Attractive appearance, can stand drugs image
- Removal of a portion of medicine from medicine boards without any effect on other well packaged medicines

BLISTER PACK

Blister packaging is a type of improvised plastic packaging generally used as unit dosage packaging for pharmaceuticals like tablets, capsules or lozenges.

Made by heating a sheet of a blister package and softening thermoplastic resin and vacuum decolorize soft sheet of plastic in a contour mold. After cooling, the sheet is released from the mold and proceeds to the filling station of the machine. It is then covered with heat sealable support material. Peel able backing material is used to meet the needs of the child resistance packaging. A material like polyester or paper is used as a component of backing lamination.

The commonly used materials for thermos formable blisters are PVC, Polyethylene combination, polystyrene and polypropylene.

STRIP PACKAGE

Strip packaging is an alternative form of pack for one unit dosage. It is a method of enclosing a related product between two webs of material so that each is contained in separate compartments. It may not be necessary for two websites of content to be identical.

Strip package unit is a form of dosage packaging which is commonly used for packaging of tablets and capsules. A strip package is formed by feeding two webs of heat which are flexible sealable by means of a hot crimping roller. The product is dropped into the pocket created earlier, making the final set of seals. The packet of constant strips normally forms. Strip packets are cut into a desired number of packets. Various packaging materials are used: paper / polyethylene / foil / PVC.

CLOSURES

The closures are the devices by which containers can be opened and closed. Proper closure of the container is essential because it prevents the loss of contents by spilling or volatilization. It protects a product from getting contaminated with dirt. This moisture prevents the degradation of the product from environmental influences such as oxygen or carbon dioxide.

Pharmaceutical closures are made from cork, glass, plastic, rubber.

SEALED TUBES

The collapsible tubes used for packaging are made of metal, plastic or lamination of foil, paper and plastic. Metal tubes are still used for products that require a high degree of barrier protection. Most of these are made of aluminum. Extruded plastic tubes are generally used for products which are compact and have limited protection of plastic.

Symbols on packaging's

Symbols on packaging's

Fragile

Keep away from sunlight

Keep away from water

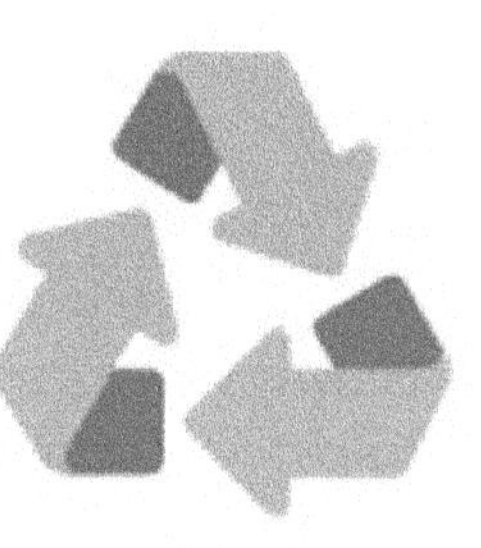

Recycle

LEGAL AND OFFICIAL REQUIREMENTS FOR CONTAINERS

FIBROUS MATERIALS

An assay that assesses the capability of container closure systems to sustain a sterile barrier against potential contaminants is known as Container Closure Integrity Testing (CCIT). Contaminants that could potentially cross a container closure barrier include micro-organisms, reactive gases and other substances (USP<1207>). Container closure systems must maintain sterility and sterility quality of final pharmaceutical, biological, and vaccine products throughout their shelf-life.

FDA Packaging Guidelines

The role of drug packaging in maintaining the standards of identity, strength, quality and purity of the drug for its intended shelf life is cited in the guidelines and references are made for direction on the nature of packaging to be utilized, to the pharmacopoeia along with tests and procedures that are to be employed.

The guidelines describe the type of containers that are utilized, dividing them into parenteral (glass or plastic) or non-parenteral containers (glass, plastic or metal) along with pressurized containers and bulk containers for active ingredients or drug products. Types of closure are also listed, for example, tamper-resistant and child-resistant caps.

Good Manufacturing Practices (GMP) similarly issues guidelines for packaging. One such example is CGMP Guideline III

IIA2 Immediate packaging containers description includes:

- Nature of material (qualitative),
- Description of closure,
- Method of opening,
- Information on container,
- Description of tamper-evidence and child-resistant closure.

Stability has to be checked for accelerated and long-term stability studies and must remain stable throughout the shelf life. The information on choice and justification of choice of containers is included in the description.

Choice of plastic include information on:

- Tightness of closure
- Protection of contents against external factors
- Interaction between the container and the preparation
- Manufacturing process influence

Justification of the choice of containers includes information on:

- Stability of active ingredient and product
- Method of administration
- Sterilizing procedures

Other specification and routine tests are performed to ensure:

- Container construction and list components
- Nature of polymers used,
- Specification of material including-

- Identification
- Visual inspection
- Dimensional test
- Physical test
- Microbial tests

STABILITY ASPECTS OF PACKAGING
FIBROUS MATERIALS

1. **Compression Strength Testing-** Packages act in a different way when they are subjected to compressive forces. In this test, the maximum quantity of compressive weight a package can hold before cracking is determined.
2. **Distribution Simulation Testing-** Packages experience many different forces during the shipping and distribution process. In this test, the manufacturer has to evaluate and document the withstanding capability of the package for distribution and storage conditions.
3. **Package Integrity Testing-** In this, verified tests are utilized to ensure the integrity of a pharmaceutical package. This test consists of dye leak test, visual inspection, vacuum leak and bubble leak testing to examine the package's integrity.

4. **Package Strength Testing-** This test is conducted to certify that the contents of the package will not detach on the application of different forces.
5. **Vibration Testing-** Goods and packages experience a range of dynamic forces and pressure that might damage the product as well as the packaging. Vibration testing is done to ensure that the package reaches the destination in good condition.
6. **Shock and Vibe Testing-** Several tests, including dropping, rotational edge dropping and rotational flat drop are performed to experience real world exposure of the package to tremor forces by fork-lifts, package handling or other factors.

QUALITY CONTROL TESTS

7. **FIBROUS MATERIALS**

- Quality Control Test for Containers
- Quality Control Test for Closures
- Quality Control Test for Secondary Packaging Materials

I. **Quality Control Test for Containers**

a. Quality control test for glass containers:

i. Hydrolytic Resistance Test- This test is only for unused glass containers.

Procedure:

- Wash the container 3 times with distilled water. Now, fill the container with the distilled water up to the filling volume.
- Heat to 100℃ for 10 minutes and allow the steam to issue from the vent cork.

- Rise the temperature from 100℃ to 121℃ over 20 minutes.
- Maintain the temperature at 121℃ to 122℃ for 60 minutes.
- Lower the temperature from 121℃ to 100℃ over 40 minutes venting to prevent vacuum.
- The instrumentation is removed from the autoclave, cools and mixes the liquids being tested.
- Test solution volume is measured in a conical flask and titrated with 0.01M HCl utilizing methyl red as an indicator.

- Blank reading is performed with water. The variance between the titration and blank denotes the volume of HCl utilized by the test mixture.

ii. Chemical Resistance Test

a. Powdered Glass Test- This test is performed to evaluate the quantity of leached alkali from the crushed glass, that generally occurs at higher temperatures. The increased amount of crushed glass results in increased quantity of leached alkali that is titrated along with 0.02 N sulphuric acid utilizing an indicator, methyl red.

Step 1: - Formulation of glass case- The containers are cleansed meticulously with distilled water and dried in clean air. Pulverize the containers in a mortar to a fine powder and move through sieve number 20 and 50.

Step 2: - Wash the case- The above sample is taken in a quantity of 10 gm into a 250mL conical flask and rinsed with 30mL acetone. The washing is repeated. The acetone is poured and dried. Later, it is utilized within 48 hrs.

Procedure:

- In 50mL of distilled water in a 250mL flask, 10 g sample is added.
- Then, it is placed in an autoclave at 121 ℃ ± 2 ℃ for 30 minutes.
- Cooled beneath running water.
- Then the solution is transferred to another flask. Washed once more with 15mL of distilled water and once more transferred.
- The sample obtained is titrated instantaneously with 0.02 N sulphuric acid with the use of an indicator, methyl red.
- The volume of the sample is documented.

b. Water Attack Test- This test is conducted on treated soda lime glass containers with limited humidity conditions that balance the surface alkali. Due to this, the glass turns chemically more resistive.

Procedure: -

- Rinse the container thoroughly with high purity water.
- Fill each container to 90% of its overflow capacity with water and is autoclaved at 121 ℃ for 30 minutes, then it is cooled and the liquid is decanted which is titrated with 0.02 N sulphuric acid utilizing the indicator, methyl red.
- The volume of sulphuric acid consumed is the measure of the number of alkaline oxides present in the glass containers.

iii. Arsenic Test- The test is used for glass vessels that are envisioned for aqueous parenteral preparations.

Procedure: -

- The internal and external surface of the container is cleansed for 5 minutes with distilled water.
- Then, the steps performed for the hydrolytic test are followed till the final combined solution is obtained.
- 10mL of the ultimate mixed volume is pipetted out and 10mL of HNO_3 is added and dried in an oven at 130 ℃.
- 10mL of hydrogen molybdate is added and refluxed for 25 minutes.
- The obtained solution is cooled and optical density is measured at 840 nm.

Limits: - The absorbance of the sample must be less than the absorbance attained using 0.1mL of arsenic standard solution (10 ppm).

b. Quality control test for plastic containers:

i. Collapsibility Test- This test is significantly utilized for containers that are to be pressed so as to remove the contents. A container falling inwards during use yields at minute 90% of its minimal contents at the specified rate of flow at the surrounding temperature.
ii. Leakage Test- 10 containers are filled with water and sealed. Then, they are upturned and kept at room temperature for 24 hours. If there is no leakage from any container, the container qualifies for the test.
iii. Clarity of aqueous extract- Select unlabeled, unmarked and non-laminated portions from suitable containers, picked randomly, enough to yield a total area of sample required, taking into account the surface area of both sides . The portions are cut into strips, none of which has a total area of more than 20cm². The strips are washed of

inessential matter by shaking them with distilled water for around 30 seconds, two to three times. Then the water is drained off.

iv. Transparency Test- Five empty containers are filled to their supposed capacity with diluted suspension. The opaqueness of the diluted suspension in each container is noticeable when viewed through the transparent containers in comparison to a similar container packed with water.

v. Water vapour permeability Test- Fill five containers with a nominal volume of water and heat seal the bottles with an aluminum foil-polyethylene laminate or other suitable seal. Weigh accurately each container and allow to stand (without any overwrap) for 14 days at a relative humidity of 60+5% and a temperature between 20 and 25 °C. Reweigh the containers. The weight deficiency in each container is less than or equal to 0.2%.

c. Quality control test for metal containers: The materials used for numerous pharmaceutical drug delivery systems include tin plated steel, mild steel, stainless steel, tin free steel, aluminum and its various alloys. For the quality control test of metal containers, 50 unfilled tubes are filled with ointment base are then vacuum-packed and kept all-night. A metal bacteriological filter put together is equipped with filter paper & heated to the melting point of the ointment base. When the preparation is liquified, the base from all tubes are squeezed at a certain rate and passed through the filter under vacuum. Later, these are washed with $CHCl_3$ and observed for particles.

II. **Quality Control Test for Closures**

a. Penetrability- This is measured to check the force required to make a hypodermic needle penetrate easily through the closure. A piercing machine is used to measure penetrability. The piercing force must not surpass a specified value. If it surpasses the specified value, the hypodermic needle can be broken as a result of unwanted hardness of the closures.

b. Fragmentation Test- This test is performed on 20 closures. All closures go colored through a piercing machine that penetrates with a hypodermic needle five times within a restricted area and the needle is cleansed to avoid transmission of any existing fragment. The contents are filtered through colored paper that contrasts with the rubber and the fragments are counted. There should be less than four fragments per unit.

c. Self-seal Ability Test- 10 vials are filled with water and enclosed with prepared closures. They are secured with a cap. For every closure, use of a fresh hypodermic needle is done. The vials are pierced 10 times, all at a diverse position. Then the vials are dipped upright in methylene blue solution (0.1%) and the peripheral pressure is reduced for about 10 minutes. The atmospheric pressure is restored and for 30 minutes, the vials are kept submerged. The outer surface of the vials is rinsed. The vials that do not comprise any trail of solution have passed the test.

d. Extractive Test-In this test, the closure is boiled with water for four hours under reflux and the water is evaporated to dryness. The residue must not surpass the stated quantity.

e. Compatibility Test- This test is performed to check the compatibility of the rubber closures with various types of substances since it is necessary to ensure there is no interaction between the matter of the container and the closure.

f. Light Absorption Test- The solution is strained across a membrane filter. Measure the light absorbance of filtrate in the range 220-360 nm using a blank solution. The absorbance must not exceed 2.0.

III. **Quality Control Test for Secondary Packaging Materials**

The test pieces of paper and board are taken for the test to be carried out in a standard condition. The temperature conditions are 23 °± 1 °C and the humidity conditions are 50% ± 2%.

a. Moisture content test- All the substances will be measured at the temperature specified for the test.

b. Folding endurance test- The test piece is folded to and fro until crack occurs.

c. Air permeability test- Important for using light weight uncoated paper on a machine having a vacuum pickup system.
d. Tensile strength test- The highest tensile strength per unit width which will withstand before breaking by a paper on plank.
e. Stiffness test- The degree of resistance offered by the board when it is bent.
f. Tear strength test- The mean strength that is needed to carry on the tearing of the first cut in a paper.
g. Burst resistance test- Evenly distributed pressure is applied at the right angles to the surface of a test paper or board that will endure even under specific requirements of the test.

www.ingramcontent.com/pod-product-compliance
Ingram Content Group UK Ltd.
Pitfield, Milton Keynes, MK11 3LW, UK
UKHW061706190726
13853UKWH00008B/2437

9 798888 498811